Twayne's English Authors Series

EDITOR OF THIS VOLUME

Kinley E. Roby

Northeastern University

Arthur Koestler

TEAS 228

Arthur Koestler

ARTHUR KOESTLER

By SIDNEY A. PEARSON, JR.
Radford College

TWAYNE PUBLISHERS
A DIVISION OF G. K. HALL & CO., BOSTON

Library of Congress Cataloging in Publication Data

Pearson, Sidney A
   Arthur Koestler.

   (Twayne's English authors series; TEAS 228)
   Bibliography: p. 161-68
   Includes index.
   1. Koestler, Arthur, 1905-   —Criticism
and interpretation.
PR6021.04Z68   828'.9'1209   77-25296
ISBN 0-8057-6699-5

For Donald and Joanne

Contents

About the Author

Sidney A. Pearson, Jr. is Chairman of the Political Science Department, Radford College, Radford, Virginia. He received his B.A. and M.A. degrees in History from the University of Maryland in 1962 and 1963 respectively. From 1963 until 1967 he served in the U.S. Marine Corps. In 1967 he returned to the University of Michigan in Political Science, receiving his Ph.D. in 1972 with a specialization in Political Theory. He taught at the University of Virginia from 1972—1977. At present he is working on a study of American Constitutional Thought in the twentieth century and American Catholic Political Thought in the twentieth century.

Preface

The work of Arthur Koestler forms a part of one of the most interesting chapters in twentieth century thought—the political, scientific, and moral thought of the secularized intellectual. The secularization of the European mind is not exclusively a phenomenon of the twentieth century. It is a process that has been underway for several centuries at least. Yet each epoch presents us with a slightly different manifestation of it. The work of Arthur Koestler is at once a unique and yet commonplace example of the twentieth century intellectual of this particular tradition.

Koestler is the author of almost thirty works—fiction, history, scientific essays, autobiography, political essays, and more. It would be impossible to consider each of these works separately. The principle aim of this study is to examine the unity within the diversity of his many writings. The intention is to show that despite what at first appears to be a bewildering diversity of Koestler's interests, there remains a basic core of thought that is present in all of them. What this core is and how it shapes Koestler's vision of the human condition in the modern world is the subject of this study.

The greatest attention is given to the fictional writing of Koestler, primarily a series of novels with a highly politicized format. Discussion of his scientific writings will also be dealt with, but not with the degree of detail as the novels. His particular views on science will be discussed within the context of their relationship to the unity of his thought as first expressed in his fiction. It is inevitable that certain of his works, fiction and nonfiction alike, will be partly or totally ignored in this study. This should not be interpreted as an implicit suggestion that they are not valuable either in their own right or as providing insight into Koestler's own thought. Rather, it is because they tend to be repetetive in terms of the basic themes developed herein. The stress of this work, therefore, is on the continuity of Koestler's work and not its remarkable diversity.

Since his first writing in the late 1930s, Koestler has been at the center of controversy. His critics and defenders have often come from the most surprising quarters. Whatever else they have said of him, no one has ever said that he was uninteresting or that he failed to touch the heart of the controversy in question. It is hoped that this relatively short study will both illuminate the central ideas of his thought that have made him so controversial and contribute to an understanding of Koestler himself. To understand Koestler aright it is necessary to see him as he sees himself and as his critics see him. I count myself among his friendly critics as one who is impressed by the depths of his insight and yet guarded about some of his conclusions. If this impression can be conveyed in this study I will count it a success.

I would like to especially thank Professor Robert Wood of the University of Virginia who read the entire manuscript version of this study and in the process contributed many helpful and insightful suggestions. Our many conversations on the various themes touched upon here have aided me far more than he could know. I would also like to thank Mr. Tony Sullivan of the Earhart Foundation in Ann Arbor, Michigan, who provided both encouragement and financial assistance for the research and writing of this study.

SIDNEY A. PEARSON, JR.

Radford College

Chronology

1905	Arthur Koestler born in Budapest, Hungary.
1922	Enrolled at the University of Vienna.
1924	Involvement in Zionist politics at Vienna.
1926	First trip to Palestine. Active in Zionism.
1927–1930	Foreign correspondent for Ullstein newspaper chain of Germany.
1930–1932	Foreign editor *B.Z. am Mittag* and science editor for *Vossiche Zeitung*.
1931	Joins German Communist party on 31 December.
1932–1933	Travels in Russia and Soviet Asia.
1936–1937	War correspondent in Spain for London *News Chronicle*. Captured by Nationalists and sentenced to death. Freed following protests in London. Publication of *Spanish Testament*.
1938	Formal break with Communist party. Editor of exile newspaper in Paris.
1939	Interned in French detention camp. *The Gladiators*.
1940	Joins French Foreign Legion.
1941	Escapes to England after fall of France. *Darkness at Noon*.
1943	*Arrival and Departure*.
1945	Special correspondent for London *Times* in Palestine. *The Yogi and the Commissar* and *Twilight Bar*.
1946	*Thieves in the Night*.
1949	*The God that Failed*, with Stephen Spender, André Gide, Louis Fischer, Richard Wright, and Ignazio Silone.
1951	*The Age of Longing*.
1952–1954	Completion of two volume autobiography, *Arrow in the Blue* and *The Invisible Writing*.
1957	Fellow of the Royal Society of Literature, England.
1959	*The Sleepwalkers*.
1964–	Fellow, Center for Advanced Study in the Behavioral

1965 Sciences, Stanford University, California. *The Act of Creation.*

1969 *The Ghost in the Machine.*

1971 *The Case of the Midwife Toad.*

1972 *The Call-Girls. First novel in over twenty years.*

1976 *The Thirteenth Tribe.*

CHAPTER 1

Portrait of a Modern Pilgrim

T HE power and the unity of Arthur Koestler's writing, fiction and
nonfiction alike, derives largely from his extraordinary ability to
make each of his separate works appear to be another missing piece in
the mosaic of modern man. It is not his style of writing, which is not
especially noteworthy, but rather the substance of it that has com-
manded such widespread attention and controversy. His work is
compelling because he has managed to make his life and ideas an
integral part of the most profound political debates of the twentieth
century. But that same dramatic quality has also proven a source of
exasperation to many readers who have denied his contention that his
case is in fact typical. His central argument on the dilemma of the
human condition—that there is no rational political solution to that
dilemma—runs counter to the most firmly held opinions of many
critics. Furthermore, although one of the most effective critics of the
political Left, Koestler never embraced the political Right in any
recognizable sense. His work is, in every sense, unique. Yet, to see in
his writing a struggle to express the enduring problems of political
man is also to see in it a tradition of political discourse that links it with
the most insightful writers in modern times. His own sense of where
he fits into the twentieth century was well stated in *The God That
Failed* in 1949:

> I became converted [to Communism] because I was ripe for it and lived in a
> disintegrating society thirsting for faith. But the day when I was given my
> Party card was merely the climax of a development which started long before
> I had read about the drowned pigs or heard the names of Marx and Lenin. Its
> roots go back to childhood; and though each of us, comrades of the Pink
> Decade, had individual roots with different twists in them, we are products
> of, by and large, the same cultural climate. It is this unity within diversity
> which makes me hope that my story is worth telling.[1]

Arthur Koestler was born in Budapest in 1905, the only child of
middle-class Jewish parents. The outbreak of World War I brought

almost instant ruin to his father's business and the family moved to Vienna where the young Koestler spent his adolescence. By his own account he was a precocious child who showed an early interest in science. That fascination with science never deserted him, although it has been overshadowed at times by a preoccupation with political issues. His scientific turn of mind led naturally to an education in the Austrian *Realschule*, which specialized in science and modern languages. In 1922 he enrolled at the Vienna Polytechnical Institute where the climate of postwar politics gradually pushed his scientific interests into the background. He acknowledged in his autobiography that he was vaguely aware of politics at an earlier age, but it was there in Vienna that his political consciousness was fully awakened in the Zionist movement among Jewish students.

Curiously, his attraction to Zionism was not accompanied by any parallel interest in Judaism as a religion. He saw Zionism not as a continuation of Jewish religion and tradition, but rather as a complete break with that past. His Old Testament roots are evident in much of the religious symbolism that pervades his writing, but it is always a detached religiosity without a sense of personal commitment by the author. On Jewish questions he always gives the impression of a pure scientist, observing phenomena from the outside. This thoroughly secular viewpoint has alternately puzzled and disturbed many of his Jewish critics who look for a greater intensity of personal commitment by a Jew on Jewish history. But it is also true that his works on specifically Jewish themes is the most vulnerable to criticism on its own merits. His least successful novel from any perspective was surely *Thieves in the Night* that dealt with the problem of political ethics on an Israeli kibbutz. Further, his controversial history of the origins of European Jewry, *The Thirteenth Tribe*, has justly been subjected to some of the most telling scholarly criticism. Only his journalistic account of the founding of the Jewish state, *Promise and Fulfillment*, the story of Palestine from 1917 to 1949, has withstood the test of time.

Koestler never formally graduated from Vienna Polytechnic. Instead, under the influence of Zionism, he went to Palestine in 1926. While there he lived on a kibbutz and participated in the early struggles to found a Jewish state in the Middle East. He drifted away from Zionism rather quickly however, and in 1927 he joined the prestigeous Ullstein chain of German newspapers as a Middle East correspondent. The Ullstein chain had the largest circulation in Germany at the time, and at the age of only twenty-two Koestler became a member of the aristocracy of European journalism. He covered the Middle East for about two years before returning to Berlin in 1930, coincidentally on the same day as the *Reichstag* fire. Working between offices in Berlin and Paris, Koestler served as science editor for *Vossiche Zeitung*, one of the Ullstein papers. While in that capacity he covered the great *Graf Zeppelin* Arctic expedition of 1931. He returned from this journalistic *coup* to widespread popular and professional acclaim and was promptly promoted to the post of foreign editor at *B.Z. am Mittag*, then Germany's largest midday newspaper. It was while he was an editor at *B.Z. am Mittag* that Koestler joined the Communist Party. When his membership was discovered by the Ullsteins in 1932, he was quietly asked to resign his newspaper post.

It is probably impossible to answer the question of whether Koestler's political world view was shaped by the Party or whether he joined the Party because of his political views. Koestler himself cannot give a definitive answer and has instead suggested the reciprocal influence of the one on the other. What is important for any student of Koestler's work is to recognize the decisive imprint his Party affiliation left on virtually all of his major writings.

He embarked on his newfound task of rebuilding the world with Marxist blueprints by leaving Europe in 1932 for that part of the edifice already under construction, the Soviet Union. After spending a year there he returned to Europe where from 1933 until 1936 he lived in conditions of extreme poverty as he wrote propaganda tracts for the Party under the tutelage of Willy Muenzenberg, at the time the most effective and prolific propagandist in the Party. Under Muenzenberg's direction, Koestler remained at the center of Party activities throughout Western Europe in the late 1930s. But if this was the period of Koestler's most active participation in the Party it was also the time when, like so many of his contemporary comrades, he began his emotionally wrenching withdrawal from the Party. Koestler's formal break with the Party came in 1938. His departure was the result of many factors that he first set forth in the enormously influential collection of similar narratives edited by Richard Crossman in 1949 under the title *The God That Failed*. Koestler followed up that essay with a more detailed version in his two volume autobiography, *Arrow in the Blue* (1952) and *The Invisible Writing* (1954), perhaps the best personal account of the European Left during that controversial epoch.

What provided the catalyst for his final and permanent rupture with the Party were his experiences in the Spanish Civil War that broke out in 1936. Koestler covered the war as a journalist traveling with several false identity cards used to conceal his Communist Party membership. The disguises failed: he was captured in 1937 by the Fascist forces under General Franco and was sentenced to death. For three months he was kept in solitary confinement, expecting at any moment to be taken from his cell and executed. It was while in solitary confinement that he discovered what he later referred to as an "oceanic sense." Many years later, in *The Act of Creation,* he described that experience as the "feeling of wonder [that] is the common source of religious mysticism, of pure science and art for art's sake; it is their common denominator and emotional bond."[2] The term itself he borrowed directly from Freud, although Koestler expanded its definition. He described the oceanic sense in several widely separate works as something akin to a religious conversion. Whatever its origins, however, it was the most important single factor in his break with the Party and with Marxist philosophy. The theme of the oceanic sense became one of the organizing principles in his most important work. Although it is most often unstated in an explicit form, its influence as a vague, semireligious symbolism is invoked repeatedly.

Koestler's break with the Party provides the critic with a convenient reference point with which to divide his life into two fairly distinct phases. The period prior to, and during, his membership in the Communist Party can be described as the activist part of his life. It was a formative period, rich in the personal adventures that later proved to be the basis for the writing that made him famous. But it was not a period of much literary productivity per se. It was only after his unexpected release from prison in Spain that he ceased to be directly involved in political life and turned toward more full-time writing. It is primarily the second phase of his career, the literary phase, that stands in need of interpretation. This second phase cannot be understood with reference to the first, but it stands apart from it for the reader who would seek to understand Koestler's work. While there is some overlap in this division, it is not misleading to describe Koestler's career in these terms.

Koestler's experiences in prison and Spain were first published in English in 1937 as *Spanish Testament* and later reissued as *Dialogue With Death.* He traveled for awhile after leaving Spain and was in Paris at the beginning of World War II. At the time of the fall of France in 1940 he was a member of the French Foreign Legion. He was again imprisoned, this time by the Vichy government, but escaped to England in 1940. At the time of his arrival in England he was already known for his successful first novel *The Gladiators* that had been published the year before. During the war year Koestler returned to his profession as a journalist with the British Broadcasting Company. It clearly marked the second phase of his career as a writer first and foremost.

The Gladiators was the first novel in his trilogy on the ethics of modern revolutions that also included *Darkness at Noon* and *Arrival and Departure*. It was this trilogy that further established Koestler's reputation as an English author, even though English was actually his third language, after Hungarian and German. During his service with the Ullstein newspapers German had become his first language for writing. *The Gladiators* was originally written in German. His second novel, *Darkness at Noon,* was also originally written in German, but the draft copy of it was lost when he fled France. The rewrite of that most famous of his novels involved its translation into English and thereafter English was to be his first literary language. *Arrival and Departure* was his first novel conceived and composed entirely in English.

The occurrence of World War II had a further impact on Koestler's reception as a writer that also helped to shape his reputation as an English author. Because of the Nazi occupation of the European continent, his first audience was almost exclusively English speaking. The explosive impact of his critique of revolutionary ideology was delayed, in France for example, until after 1945. For Americans and throughout the English-speaking world, however, the impact was more immediate. As an exposé of Stalinism and as an explanation of the infamous Moscow Purge Trials of the 1930s, Koestler set the tone for much of the postwar debate on the nature of Communism. Throughout the remainder of the 1940s and into the 1950s, *Darkness at Noon* and its controversial author were at the center of the political storm that raged over an interpretation of the role of intellectuals under Communism. It became virtually impossible to ignore *Darkness at Noon* in the prolonged debate, and the ideological battle lines between the Left and the Right were often drawn with reference to how one stood in relation to the challenge Koestler had thrown down. The reception of Koestler in France is especially telling. When *Darkness at Noon* was translated and published as *Le Zero et l'Infini* it was apparently one of the factors that left to the animosity between Jean-Paul Sartre and Albert Camus. Sartre had argued against its publication because it was true while Camus had argued for its appearance precisely for the same reason. It was a significant factor among many intellectuals in the vote against a French Communist government, although its influence among the electorate as a whole is problematic.

Although it is with reference to his political novels, essays and autobiography—all dealing basically with what he has called the "Pink Decade" of the 1930s—that Koestler is best known, there has been more to his writing than that alone. He bid a tentative farewell to politics in 1955 with the publication of a collection of his essays in *The Trail of the Dinosaur*. The literary phase of his career also includes a provocative trilogy on the metaphysical roots of modern science and his interpretation of the meaning of the post-Newtonian revolution in modern science: *The Sleepwalkers* (1959), *The Act of Creation* (1964), and *The Ghost in the Machine* (1969). Here, as with his political works, Koestler generated controversy from the outset. His apparently heretical notions about the origins of scientific creativity met with a much smaller audience than had his discussion of revolutionary ethics, but the ensuing debate was no less heated because of a comparatively smaller number of participants. Indeed, the acrimony surrounding his scientific writing closely rivaled and in some ways was parallel to the earlier controversies. In 1972 Koestler seized upon this similarity and combined the interaction of modern science with politics in one of his best and surely his wittiest novel, *The Call-Girls*.

Whether or not Koestler's life and writings are really representative of the modern intellectual pilgrim is not the primary issue in evaluating his work. That aspect of the debate on his work is at best a distraction and at worst serves only to divert attention from the substance of his message. There can be little doubt that he addressed himself to some of the most serious and problematic questions of modern man. And he did so not on the periphery of the debate, but often at the very center of it. Partly as a consequence of this, his best and most controversial writing is not bound to the particular historical setting of the "Pink Decade." It consistently relates to the tension between the particular and the general properties of the human condition. The result in his works is a rare synthesis between the unique and the universal. Through the numerous volumes of his writings he has both aided his readers in interpreting the world and contributed to its intellectual shape.

CHAPTER 2

Between the Yogi and the Commissar

FACED with a political choice he perceived to be limited to Fascism on the one hand and Communism on the other, on New Year's Eve in 1931, Arthur Koestler chose Communism. That choice has marked the content, the form, and the purpose of his most dramatic fiction. Years later he recalled the choice not as a reluctant one between two evils, but as a positive commitment to good over evil. It was, he wrote, more in the nature of a religious conversion than a question of pragmatic politics. He saw the beginning of the new year and the joining of the German Communist Party as a mystical union of the symbolic and the practical that was to be the beginning of a new life. Whatever else his association with Communism may have done, it has had the unmistakable effect of giving to almost all of his writing an intensely politicized focus. The complex array of motivations that lay behind that choice, along with his agonizing decision to leave the party in 1938, have ever since shaped the ordering principles of his work.

Koestler's experience with Communism during what has come to be called the "Red Decade" of the 1930s followed a pattern similar to that of many other intellectuals at the time. It was a career marked first by enthusiastic conversion, followed by varying degrees of disillusionment that often resulted in a splinter group heresy, such as Trotsky, or else a complete political apostasy, as with Koestler. Although the personal stories were as diverse as the personalities behind them, there was also a unity within that diversity that sparked the intense political arguments that surrounded the Communist party during the decade. The structure of the debates was much the same for the true believers within the party as for its enemies without—the relationship of theory to practice in revolutionary politics. When Koestler joined the debate toward the end of the

17

decade with his powerful fiction, he managed to crystalize the essence of the problem for the opposing forces with a clarity that made him one of the central participants in the ideological struggle. By casting the revolutionary dilemma as a conflict between ends and means in his novels he seemed to have stated the arguments everyone else was grasping to articulate but had somehow not quite found the proper words.

The political dilemma of modern revolutions, as Koestler articulated it, was a question of means vs. ends. When, if ever, does the end desired justify the means necessary to reach that end? And if the end itself cannot justify the means, whatever will? For converts, heretics, apostates, and enemies alike, this was viewed by many to be the heart of the revolutionary problem of the 1930s. Koestler proved to be one of the intellectual catalysts that brought this dilemma clearly to the fore.

It has become commonplace in describing the affiliation of so many intellectuals with Communism during this period to say that they were "duped" by the party and Stalin due to their political naivete. Koestler however, most honest than most, has never accepted this rationalization. "We were not blind", he wrote some years later.[1] What Koestler and many of his contemporaries had consciously accepted in politics was the primacy of ends over means. His contemporary, Stephen Spender, wrote at the time that since the ends of Communism cannot be achieved immediately "it is all the more necessary that people should exist only for the ends." That end of which he saw the party as represenative was "an unpolitical age."[2] The ultimate abolition of politics from the human condition was the final goal. The first mass disillusionment among the intellectuals as a class came during the infamous Moscow Show Trials of the late 1930s. The terror in Stalin's Russia called into question the proposition that politics, meaning in essence conflict, could in fact be eliminated.

For Koestler the problem was an intensely personalized one, because he had worked directly within the party bureaucracy and knew it first hand as did few of the heretics and apostates who later recorded their experiences. It was one of the major strengths of his writing that he captured in it the bureaucratic mentality of the Soviet Union so faithfully. In addition, Koestler has always tended to view his own life as a miniature version of the spiritual and political cross-currents of modern Europe in general. This gives to all of his work and impression of autobiographical flavor that is the key to much of its fascination. But it is also a quality that has earned him considerable criticism.[3] At its most insightful level, it is what has made his work so compelling. The argument over ends and means never seems to be an intellectual abstraction. It is always tied specifically to his personal actions in the party. It is the intensity of his internalized struggle that has helped to make his work timeless.

To explain this intensity, Koestler has seen within himself a Faustian urge to "know" through personal experience the totality of the world around him. He has regarded this urge as the source of his creative writing where he has attempted to recreate those experiences. He has described it as a compulsion "to achieve identity between the subject who knows and the object of its knowing."[4] To write at all, he says of himself, is to write a history of himself as a reflection of the history of twentieth century Europe.

I   *The Structure of Modern Politics in Koestler*

Koestler's vision of politics in the twentieth century is comparatively narrow when contrasted with some others, such as an Orwell or a Silone, for example. But what it often lacks in breadth it more than compensates for in precision and clarity of those objects brought under his scrutiny. These objects are the practical and theoretical dilemmas of political choice in a century dominated by revolution. Revolutions in general, and the Marxist revolutions in particular, he saw as set against a particular historical backdrop that paralleled his own intellectual dispositions.

The most distinguishing features of Koestler's political landscape revolve around the Bolshevik Revolution in Russia and the rise of Fascism on the one hand, and the role of science in modern society on the other. Practical choices among competing political ideologies in the 1930s, he argued, were limited to Communism and Fascism. More liberal forms of democratic government, such as prevailed at the time in the English-speaking world and a few other enclaves, scarcely enter his political picture. The political clashes in his work are those between the most incompatible and diametrically opposite forces. There is seldom a middle ground.[5]

At times it is difficult to tell whether or not Fascism and Communism are really political opposites for Koestler. The evidence in his work is ambiguous. In some of his later writing, it appears that they are both manifestations of the same nonpolitical phenomenon— the collapse of Christianity in particular and of religion in general as the transcendent ordering principle of Western civilization. The "death of God" and the loss of religious faith are conspicuously recurring themes that appear in his work from beginning to end. In this context, Marxism often seems to be merely the most symbolically developed example of the thoroughly secularized vision of politics in the contemporary world. Marxism as a secularized religion corresponds to his own self-interpretation and to the appeals of Communism to his generation of intellectuals. The supposedly nonalienated man of Marxism was to be realized through political action in concert with other men as opposed to an individual act or gratuitous grace from God. In *The Age of Longing*, for example, he describes the nature of this transformation by contrasting religious faith with its political counterpart as an ordering principle. The goal, never realized by Koestler, of these secular movements is to bring into harmony the material and spiritual life of mankind. Such a goal, if realized, would by its very nature abolish politics and usher in an "unpolitical age."

In terms of political theory, the overriding problem for Marxist theoreticians was the translation of theory into practice. The question had been precisely stated by Marx in his "Eleventh Thesis on Feuerbach," in which he wrote: "The philosophers have only *interpreted* the world, in various ways; the point, however, is to change it."[6] For scientific revolution in the Marxist scheme of things, the validity of the theory came to depend on its ability to predict events consistant with the theory and combine them with a political activism based on that theory. What the Marxists called *praxis*, the transformation of theory into practice, was the political problem of revolution. This in turn raised the issue of ends verses means in revolutionary activism.

The practical model for this dilemma in all of Koestler's early writing is the Soviet Union under Stalin. There were no other Communist models at the time from which to derive examples of the relation of theory to practice. By the late 1930s it had become painfully obvious to Koestler that the Russian Revolution had not solved the central problem of praxis as he saw it—the dilemma of ends and means. The rise of Stalin and Hitler, for example, seemed to run counter to the Marxist argument that individuals were relatively unimportant in determining the course of history. The Moscow trials brought the problem to a head in the late 1930s at the time Koestler began to write. It was a fortuitous blend of the man with his time that helped to launch Koestler into such a conspicuous spot in the debate that was then raging over the question of praxis in Marxism. It is not an exaggeration to say that Koestler as much as any other single person altered the structure of that debate by his writing. After the appearance of his second novel, *Darkness at Noon*, it was virtually impossible to discuss the Russian Revolution without reference to Koestler's thesis—that the revolution had been doomed from beginning because of the iron political law that revolutions fail whenever either ends or means dominates the other.

With the Soviet Union as the principal guide for intellectuals in politics, Koestler faced the problem of drawing universal laws from a regime that was historically unique in every respect. It was a gigantic laboratory where the theories of Marx and Lenin were being tried out. Koestler recognized from the beginning what so many had been loath to admit even to themselves, that acceptance of the revolution meant an eyes open embrace of tyranny. In *The State and Revolution*, Lenin had written: "Only he is a Marxist who *extends* the recognition of the class struggle to the recognition of the dictatorship of the proletariat."[7] And was not the party the living embodiment of that dictatorship and Stalin the historically necessary head of the party? Only if the party's claims were somehow not true could the question of ends and means be brought up. When Koestler made ends verses means the central issue of his work it announced his break with the party.

What had come to most trouble Koestler was the determinism of Marxism at the theoretical level that had made the problem of ends and means on the practical level so acute. Marxist revolution in the twentieth century had revealed, without providing any solution, the dilemma of the human condition in the twentieth century. On a practical level, that of politics, it was the conflict between "noble ends and ignoble means," but at a much deeper level it was the failure of nineteenth century conceptions of science to be translated into a program for social action in the twentieth century. As late as 1943, Koestler wrote that Marx and Engels remain "the truest and profoundest guide to the last century."[8] What is to be noted, however, is that they are only the most profound guides to the last century. In the twentieth century they have become dangerous anachronisms. The dictatorship of the proletariat, he argues, whatever it may have meant in the context of the nineteenth century, means unbridled tyranny in the twentieth century. To the extent that it is necessary to believe in the dictatorship of the proletariat in order to be a Marxist, Koestler had ceased to be one. But the problem of revolution does not end there. Determinism in scientific thought is the submerged portion of the iceburg in Marxism that needs to be challenged.

The strength of Marx's theories lay in his ability to combine an understanding of science with a vision of politics. Since Marx, one could not be an intellectually respectable revolutionary without this combination. It formed the rational basis for the notion of praxis. In turn, Marxists were the only coherent, organized revolutionaries who had such a praxis. Koestler early discovered that one could not raise the question of ends and means alone within the revolutionary model. To raise that issue was to call into question a whole range of assumptions about the nature of the human condition that were inarticulated and largely hidden from view. As a result, it was from his critique of revolutionary praxis in Marxism that eventually informed the basis of his larger world view in later work. It forms the core of understanding his work as a whole and in detail.

The basic structure of politics, as Koestler experienced it and as he saw in the larger historical map of Europe in the twentieth century, was the irrationality of choice that in the final analysis was reduced to either ends or means. One could, he said, have an ethic of one or the other, but not both at the same time. Their opposition was diametrical and not dialectical; there was no synthesis. The essence of the human condition in politics is thus reduced to what he considers to be a draconian choice between two separate ethical systems, neither of which can rightly claim to embody the totality of ethical imperatives. It is a choice between expediency on the one hand and morality on the other.[9] It is, nevertheless, a choice that cannot be avoided. To face the challenge of the modern world is to confront this dilemma. It is a conflict, he has repeatedly stated, which "is not an invention of the philosophers, but a conflict we face at each step in our daily lives."[10] The choice between morality as means and expediency as end is reflected in the political life of each individual. In this way, political society is man writ large and the dilemma of the individual is the dilemma of the revolutionary state.

This dilemma of the human condition, the problem of ends and means, is inherently insoluable in Koestler's work. As it informs his theory of the nature of revolutionary regimes, it means that no revolution can either overcome or transcend the dilemma. But this condition is also one that invokes a Promethian defiance of the gods who placed mankind in this seemingly intolerable predicament. An integral part of this condition for Koestler thus becomes a search for a rational way out of it even while accepting the impossibility of such an escape. It is Koestler's version of a rational Prometheus.

II   *The Yogi and the Commissar*

The symbolism Koestler chose to express this dilemma of ends and means is that of the yogi and the commissar. They are represenative types of man who are assigned opposite ends of the political spectrum. Symbolically, they are the logical conclusions of the ends-means argument. At one end of this continuum is the yogi, who represents the political ethic of pure means. At the other extreme is the commissar, who embodies the ethic of pure ends. The world of political decisions in Koestler's imagery is conducted along this continuum, which is always dominated by these mutually exclusive figures. In the final analysis, political choices are defined by either the yogi or the commissar and not by any blending of the two.

The yogi believes that means alone count in politics and that all efforts to justify political actions must focus exclusively on those means. For the yogi mentality there is no social change except that which follows from a change in the soul of an individual. He takes it for granted that the ends of everything human in origin are unpredictable and hence that there can never be a rational theory of society that is future-oriented. The future is an unknown quantity. It does not follow from this that Koestler's yogi is a moral relativist when confronted with a political choice. Rather, what he argues is that reason alone cannot be an effective guide in politics; the closer man approaches to absolute truth, the more likely reason is to fail as a guide. It is a mentality that disposes the yogi toward passivity in politics. No forms of political activity move him to action, regardless of the specific issues involved. Injustice, tyranny, wars, opression of any kind or from any quarter—all are matters of political indifference. His sense of morality is strictly internalized. The only thing that matters to him is truth, or the absolute, to which he feels a mystical attachment by a sort of invisible umbilical cord. Political action threatens to break this cord and hence is shuned as the supreme evil.

At the other end of this idealized spectrum stands the pure form of the commissar. He is the mirror image of the yogi in every respect. He is the supreme political activist for whom all political morality must be structured with exclusive reference to the end sought. To him it is the end alone that matters, and everything that serves that end is by definition moral. He further believes that there is no such thing as permanence in the human condition. Everything is in a constant state of change and flux. There is no defect in human character or institutions that cannot be changed by the proper application of socio-political engineering techniques. By implication, there is a "scientific" answer to every problem in the human condition. That answer is a deterministic one that sees events strictly from within a cause-effect relationship. Because he believes that any end can be realized, he also tends to believe that it "must" be achieved. As a theoritician of ends, he is exclusively futuristically oriented. He would never admit that the future may be opaque and unpredictable. He is, in short, a revolutionary whose politics are predicated on his vision that an earthly paradise can and will take concrete form in the here and now. In Marxist terms, it is the unity of theory and practice in a comprehensive praxis.

The commissar's determinism is a product of his mechanistic notions of science born of the nineteenth century's wedding of Newton with social philosophy. It is not science per se that is the villain of the piece for Koestler, but rather the identification of science with its Newtonian form. In his early writing, Koestler concentrated on the political manifestations of this mechanistic view of the human condition. Here his writing was primarily fictional and concerned specifically with Marxist revolution. Later, after the mid-1950s, Koestler turned increasingly to a consideration of the theoretical structure of modern science that lay behind the commissar's politics. During this phase of Koestler's writing he shifted away from fiction and toward nonfiction as the method by which he developed his views.

In Koestler's scheme of political reality, practical politics is ultimately the monopoly of these two ideal types. Whenever any political theory is pressed to its logical conclusion, there is no other alternative than the yogi or the commissar. This does not mean that there are no other political philosophies than these two. On the contrary, Koestler says, the history of the modern world is littered with the debris of political ideologies that have tried to steer between these two extremes. But these are "halfway houses," as he calls them, soft efforts to avoid the hard choices of real politics. They are symptomatic of an intellectual failure in the modern world to genuinely understand the nature of the human condition.

Those social movements that are informed by these halfway houses are little more than points along the arc of a pendulum that in its unceasing swing favors first one side and then the other without distinction. In the twentieth century that pendulum has swung to the side of the commissar, the embodiment of the major challenges of our time. The tragedy of this dichotomy is that there can be no true agreement or understanding between the extremes, because they share no common ground. Such debate as appears rational to the halfway house intellectuals is founded on an illusion. "The argument will lead nowhere", he notes, "for the real issue remains. . .between fundamental conceptions, of Change from Without and Change from Within."[11]

Participation in politics, which is the essence of the message in Koestler's early political fiction writing, means to choose fatefully between ends and means. In one sense, the inaction of the yogi only appears possible in the abstract. In reality, the yogi's illusions have as great an effect on politics as do those of the commissar. This is because his abnegation of political responsibility abandons the world to the mercy of commissar types. At a practical level, therefore, everyone is compelled by the nature of things to take responsbility for not only what they do but also for whatever they may fail to do. The moral structure of Koestler's world view is that each individual is responsible for his political choices even though the dilemma posed by those choices is not of his own making. In the background then is an inscrutable and irrational universe that bears the final responsibility for the human predicament.

III   *The Dilemmas of Determinism in Koestler*

The problem of determinism versus indeterminism is one of the important but sometimes subtle themes in Koestler's work. It is closely tied to the problem of the yogi and the commissar and of science in the modern world, but it deserves separate consideration here. This is because the dilemma of determinism in its ethical dimension is one of the great stumbling blocks in Koestler's world view. It is the greatest source of inconsistency in his work and hence has often been the greatest source of misunderstanding in the interpretation of his work even when determinism itself was not obviously the issue in question.

The problem is crucial for the outcome of the yogi-commissar debate since it influences for Koestler the question of responsibility for political actions. If the commissar is correct that the course of history is determined in the Marxist sense, then it follows logically that he is no more than an instrument of the forces of history. The result is that he is ultimately absolved of any personal guilt for any crimes committed by the revolutionary terror. This is intolerable to Koestler and the grounds for much of his rejection of revolution. But, on the other hand, if men really are the free-willed creatures alleged by the yogi, then and only then can individual responsibility be restored. His problem is that while he has personally rejected the commissar's politics in practice, he does not reject them entirely in theory. His writing reflects a search for exactly that halfway house in political philosophy that the structure of his dilemma suggests is impossible.

Koestler is fully aware of the debate over determinism and indeterminism in the revolutionary notions of praxis. He left the party in large measure because he felt a strong sense of personal guilt for the revolutionary terror during his tenure in the party. Yet he could never wholly reject the idea of impersonal historical forces that shape and form the context of individual actions. His response was to construct his own version of a mystical halfway house from which he could criticize both the yogi and the commissar. But, by his own definition, such a stance took him outside of the role of an active participant in politics and rendered it a passive, yogi-type role: "Astrology is founded on the belief that man is formed by his cosmic environment: Marx held that he is the product of his social environment. I believe both propositions to be true."[12]

Such statements as this have given to Koestler's work at crucial junctures a certain mystical quality that seems to stand in sharp contrast with his overall rationalism. It is accurate to observe, as most of his critics have, that Koestler is first and foremost a rationalist in his writing. His heroes are always reasoned ideas rather than people. But that is only a part of the picture. There is also a strong undercurrent of the irrational constantly threatening to surface. And when on occasion the irrational does appear, it is often in the form of an occult mysticism. This conflict between reason and unreason is tied to the problem of the yogi and the commissar as mirror opposites of each other. Evidently this tension also mirrors much of Koestler's own intellectual conflict. But even more importantly, if the question is raised as to whether Koestler is really a Marxist or an anti-Marxist, a yogi or a commissar, a revolutionary or a reactionary, the answer will depend upon which level the question is addressed. At the practical level, there is no doubt but that Koestler has written some of the most powerful indictments of revolution in his time. But at the more theoretical level, his repudiation of the commissar ethic is quite ambiguous.

This ambiguity is born of his rejection of a deterministic science that the commissar represents but at the same time of an acceptance of the primacy of ends over means on the political level under limited circumstances. Politically, he has said, the end does justify the means whenever the social experiments are practiced on a small scale and "the results predictable with reasonable certainty."[13] Ruthlessness, he then goes on to say, when administered in small quantities, is a stimulant to the body politic despite its propensity to prove fatal when administered in large doses. "A certain admixture of ruthlessness is inseparable from human progress."[14] But surely this explanation for the occasional necessity for the commissar ethic cannot end here. Short of the death of the patient, Koestler offers little to inform his reader as to what might be "too much" or "too little" ruthlessness. This lack of clarity in distinguishing when he is talking about theory and when he is addressing himself to the practice of politics in the human condition has led some critics to regard him as a theoretical Marxist even after leaving the party.[15]

Determinism versus indeterminism thus becomes as much of a moral consideration in Koestler's work as a practical problem. In a fundamental sense, the issue is never resolved. He is a determinist to the extent that he believes in progress and the necessity of politics to provide the engine for that progress. He never sides with the yogi on the theoretical plane. Yet he is often painfully aware that within his scheme of reality it is the yogi who represents morality, and Koestler's critique of revolutionary ethics is nothing if not an exercise in moral condemnation of revolutionaries. The arguments of his novels, essays, and histories are pitched to two different levels—the theoretical and the practical. There is a tension between the two that is a product of the problem of the unity of theory and practice in Marxism. It means that as Koestler constantly rehashes the arguments over praxis with the commissars in his novels, it is never entirely clear which one wins.

The problem that comes through again and again in all of Koestler's work is that the problems of the human condition in the twentieth century are primarily rooted in a failure of theory and ideas. This does not mean that action is ignored in his work. The practical consequences of theoretical decisions confronts the reader at every turn. But action in his novels tends to be highly abstract in form and its function is chiefly to highlight discrepancies between theory and practice.

The greatest danger of the commissar to those who would question his actions is that at the theoretical level it is he alone in the contemporary world who is in manipulative controls of the symbols of the future. The symbolic construction of the future is ordered in a deterministic fashion that makes his arguments for the primacy of ends seem plausible. Critics are forced to oppose him on both levels of theory and practice but are at a distinct disadvantage in doing so. Koestler sees such criticism as consigned to a sort of endless political purgatory. Without ever really losing the argument, he never wins it either.

Perhaps the major importance in Koestler's critique of the commissar's determinism is in the impact it had in the 1940s in the debate over the origins and results of the Red Decade. By arguing that determinism was the fatal flaw in the commissar mentality, it also meant that his critique of revolution went beyond a mere criticism of Stalin for having "betrayed" the revolution, such as Trotsky, for example, had made. The commissar type, in Koestler's view, could not renounce determinism because the entire structure of his notion of praxis would collapse. It was, therefore, the fate of revolutions to fail. The revolutionary construction of symbols of the future were products of an imagination that had been formed in the nineteenth century, when Newtonian science was the paradigm. In the modern world, however, since Einstein in particular, science was better understood as probabilistic rather than deterministic. Since determinism was a scientific error, its political application in Russia doomed the revolution from its origins in the minds of the revolutionaries. It was the entire commissar-revolutionary tradition that was flawed rather than specific individuals within it.

IV   *The Place of Psychology in Revolution*

The portrait of the revolutionary personality that emerges in Koestler's fiction is that of a commissar who consistently fails to measure up to the image of the ideal type. He is one who is striving after what is in practice and unattainable goal. The result is that "the evidence suggests that twentieth-century man [the commissar] is a political neurotic."[16] For the commissar, whether he accepts it or not, "the concept of free choice is implicit in all systems of moral values and ethical imperatives."[17] It is the rupture between theory and practice in revolutionary politics that has caused this neurosis.

If political man appears to Koestler as a neurotic, this view is in part derived from Koestler's particular structure of reason. Reason in Koestler's work shows unmistakable signs, whether consciously realized or not, of being patterned after the structure of reason in the work of Kant. There is an intense and unrelenting conflict between the real and the ideal. But, unlike Kant, it is not clear whether the "real" is to be understood as the theoretical or the practical nor which is "ideal." The origin of the conflict is never entirely clear in Koestler's work. Sometimes it appears as if the social environment is the cause of the rupture of praxis that breeds neurotic men. At other times it appears as purely the result of the individual projecting out onto the world around him his own neurotic predispositions. In his autobiography, Koestler wrote, "It is not Marxist theory itself which turns people into rebels but a psychological disposition that makes them susceptable to revolutionary theories."[18] In *Darkness at Noon*, on the other hand, he seems to imply that it is the logic of ideas that is responsible for molding the revolutionary personality rather than the other way around.

Political man in the twentieth century is a neurotic personality because of his inability to reconcile theory with practice. The underlying conflict between determinism and indeterminism that has surfaced in the twentieth century has torn the practice of politics asunder. For Koestler this represents an intellectual crisis of the first magnitude. And because it is an intellectual crisis, it is among intellectuals that the problem must be studied and analyzed. The practice of politics cannot be made wholly rational until the real and the ideal are brought into harmony, and this in turn can only be the end result of an act of reason. The problem of revolutionary praxis in the Bolshevik Revolution is due to the sort of "treason of the intellectuals" that Julien Benda had described.

In his novels of the 1940s, Koestler had tried to describe the general characteristics of political neurosis, but had done so in a more or less haphazard manner. In 1953, his essay, "A Guide to Political Neurosis," represented his first attempt to describe systematically what he saw as its main features.[19] The intellectual's allegiance to the programs of the commissar begins with a distorted universe of science in which no facts are admitted that do not conform to the internal consistancies of the commissar's paradigm of revolution. Koestler caricatures this trait among certain intellectuals—savagely in *The Age of Longing*, and with somewhat greater subtlety in his last novel, *The Call-Girls*. It is a trait that he recognizes as reminiscent of his own experiences in the party.[20] It results in what he calls a "private Iron Curtain" inside the skull of the true believer. The realities of practical experience tend to be ignored, while the realities of imagination are substituted in a symbolic transformation. This precarious balance between experience and imagination is always in danger of being upset by the constant intrusion of practical facts. The intrusion of these facts, however, does not always result in changes in theory but is at least as likely to result in attempts to change the facts themselves.

This then is the pattern of thought for the modern intellectual fellow traveler of the commissar. Systematically unable to learn from their past, they create "wish-dreams" about the future and develop improbable arguments over ends and means that are a form of escape from what he sees as the reality of man's common condition. These wish-dreams of a social paradise in Russia constitute the bane of rational discussion.

Destructive though the commissar's politics may be, it does conform to a psychological reality of an even deeper order in Koestler's opinion. These wish-dreams have become a substitute for religious meaning. Koestler himself had flirted with Zionism in his youth as a student in Vienna before finally rejecting it. One of the subtle and often unnoticed themes that runs from Koestler's first novel to the last is his understanding of the loss of religious faith and of the ways in which the commissar's ideology has become a surrogate religion. "Twentieth-century man is a political neurotic because he has no answer to the question of the meaning of life, because socially and metaphysically he does not know where he 'belongs.' "[21]

The unprecedented authority that the commissar has come to hold over the minds of men is caused by the near total collapse of the spiritual world represented by the yogi and by traditional Western religion. We have not, he says, fully digested either the meaning of that past or what the modern break with it truly means. The challenge of our time is to come to grips with the meaning and implications of the break. Unless that challenge is successfully met, he notes that as a species we may go the way of the dinosaur. He became a Communist, he wrote, because he "was ripe for it and lived in a disintegrating society thirsting for faith."[22]

The paradox is that it is technology that has dealt the death blow to the place of religion in man's life and as a result has made the most technologically advanced societies the most neurotic and therefore prone toward the commissar. The yogi mentality is a more primitive one and tends to be most noticable in underdeveloped regions of Europe and in the non-Western world. It is the veneer of scientific knowledge by the masses that saturates Western culture with the notion that science, understood as progressive and deterministic, will solve all the dilemmas of modern life. The argument that the end will justify the means strikes a responsive chord with them. It is a reflection of our own intellectual weakness, he writes, "that though we reject it, we have not found a complete answer to it."[23] The commissar is future-oriented in the same way as the masses have become future-oriented. He can symbolize in his revolutionary ideology their lost eschatological faith. "Devotion to pure Utopia, and revolt against a polluted society, these are the two poles which provide the tension of all militant creeds."[24]

V The Unity and Order of Koestler's Work

The problem of ends and means, symbolized by the twin images of the yogi and the commissar and by the scientific and psychological implications that surround that problem, is the central organizing principle of Koestler's writing. This is especially true as had long been recognized of his earlier writing, but it is also true of his later work, which fact has not always been fully understood. The reasons why the continuity in Koestler's work has not always been appreciated is twofold. First, his early career, from the publication of *The Gladiators* in 1939 until the completion of his two volume autobiography in 1954, was dominated by political novels and essays. After the mid-1950's, however, Koestler turned his attention increasingly to the history, paradigms, and consequences of modern science in the post-Newtonian world. On the surface this has given the impression of two fairly distinct writing phases, and most have tended to see his career as divided along these lines. Second, and closely related to the first tendency, most critics of his political fiction and essays were so absorbed with the immediate question of the revolution in the Soviet Union that they failed to perceive the deeper questions in his work. When Koestler later turned to popularizing scientific thought with his own interpretations, many saw this as an abandonment of his earlier political concerns. Koestler himself, in several statements, gave some weight to this view but it is misleading if not wholly inaccurate. It was built on a failure to appreciate the close connection Koestler saw in his first novels between the politics and the scientific vision of the commissar.

There is unity in Koestler's work, both fiction and nonfiction, that goes deeper than the symbolization of the human condition in terms of the yogi and the commissar. Behind that symbolic construction lies the greater problem of knowledge and the role of reason in human affairs. Taken as a whole, Koestler's writing may be described as a search for an objectively truthful and rational conception of the human condition that is independent of that condition. What the sum of Koestler's writing obliquely points toward is an ancient question—is there, in the final analysis, any objective measure of truth that is not merely an illusion or the shadow on the wall of a Platonic cave? As with so many points in his work, any answer he gives in usually tenuous or ambiguous at best. In all of his direct statements, he gives every indication that he believes such reasoned truth as man knows is the result of a Promethian defiance of nature. The very conception of the yogi and the commissar, after all, is an attempt to render the irrational as rational. But none of his work reflects the latent nihilism that has dominated so much of the modern temper. In spite of his rejection of religion, there is also in it a search for a rational faith that a rationalist such as himself can believe.

To read Koestler's work as he intended it to be read requires that the dilemma of the yogi and the commissar be kept firmly in mind. It shapes and directs all of the ideological outcomes of his fiction. But more than that, it further influences so much of his nonfictional writing as to be easily misunderstood without it as a guide. Because of this overriding importance of the dilemma of ends and means in revolutionary ethics for Koestler's work, it is appropriate to concentrate any study of his work on those pieces where this dilemma is most closely argued. In his later writing, it is often more implicit than explicit.

Koestler's arguments on the dilemmas of revolutionary ethics were developed primarily in a trilogy of novels that appeared from 1939 through 1943—*The Gladiators, Darkness at Noon,* and *Arrival and Departure.* He followed up these novels with two others—*Thieves in the Night* in 1946 and *The Age of Longing* in 1951. *Thieves in the Night* was an attempt to consider the ethics of survival in the modern world by relating a fictional account of an Israeli kibbutz. It was perhaps his least successful novel from a purely literary perspective, and its story need not be extensively considered in any discussion of his work that aims to understand the heart of his politics. *The Age of Longing,* on the other hand, does wrap up very well many of the general points from his trilogy on revolution. It is a crucial work in his transition as a writer from fiction to nonfiction. Only after his political fiction has been understood in its proper context can his nonfiction trilogy on the science of the mind—*The Sleepwalkers, The Act of Creation,* and *The Ghost in the Machine*—be seen as a continuation of his early career.

Science is not an interest that is divorced from the dilemma of the yogi and the commissar but rather a direct outgrowth of it. A scientific world view is what provides a rational substructure to the commissar's politics. To call that particular view into question was what required Koestler to go beyond the dilemma of the yogi and the commissar and yet bound him closely to that concept.

CHAPTER 3

The Law of Detours

ARTHUR Koestler's first novel on the dilemma of ends and means in revolutionary ethics was entitled *The Gladiators* and appeared in 1939. It is a fictionalized account of the Spartacus slave uprising against Rome during the first century B.C. The historical setting is unique among Koestler's works and plays a dual role in its symbolism. First of all, because the commissar is the dominant modern type, with his emphasis on ends, to deal with the problem of means as does *The Gladiators* seems to call for an historical setting. Second, the figure of Spartacus had considerable symbolic appeal to the self-styled revolutionaries of the 1920s and 1930s. He was a semimythical figure who was portrayed most often as the incarnation of spontaneous revolution for all the instinctively right reasons. Koestler's deliberate reversal of this view of Spartacus was sufficient in itself to make the novel controversial among party members and fellow travelers.

The basic argument of *The Gladiators* is to present half of the yogi-commissar dilemma. Koestler has already developed in his own mind the notion that all revolutions invariably fail. But they do not all fail for the same reasons. What if, he asks of those revolutionary critics of the Soviet Union who saw in Stalin the reason for the failure of the revolution, the revolution had taken a different course? What if a revolutionary movement were to allow the means to dominate the ends? Would such a moral stance make any difference in the success or failure of the revolution? His answer, that although it would affect the outcome of the revolution it would not affect the success or failure of it, was in itself a startling thesis. Revolutions were doomed to failure no matter what they do.

The choice of Rome as the setting for his first novel also served Koestler in two additional and subtle ways. It allowed him to explore the dilemma of ends and means in such a way as to suggest that its relevance was not dependent upon the particular circumstances of twentieth century revolutions. As an inescapable truth of the human condition, it was applicable to all men at all times. Further, reading the story from the perspective of the twentieth century, the contemporary reader cannot help but be aware that elsewhere in the Roman Empire prophets are heralding the immanent arrival of Christ. While Koestler only hints at this Christological symbolism in places, it is a fundamental and often overlooked theme of *The Gladiators*. A new civilization is about to be born at the very moment when things appear to be most bleak to wholly secularized mankind. Furthermore, the immanent transformation of the world owes nothing to the revolt of Spartacus. It is an event over which men have no control as it originates in another dimension of reality altogether. It forms a part of Koestler's mythical union of astrology and reason. The theme of the "new god" about to be born is one that runs throughout Koestler's fiction and nonfiction alike. And to develop that theme he constantly returns to a Christological symbolism that is unique in modern literature.

The Gladiators was published approximately a year after Koestler formally broke with the Communist party. If the reader looks at it with a Marxist eye for criticism, it will be noted immediately that this is not a proletarian novel within the meaning of that term in the climate of opinion at that time. This observation is meant to suggest that Koestler's break with the party in psychological terms, as opposed to the merely formal separation in 1938, was more decisive and came earlier than many of his critics have assumed. In *The Gladiators*, the reader is not led to identify with the struggling masses, who are usually presented as little more than bruitish louts, but instead with the logic of the abstract ideas behind the revolt. The personalities in the novel are wooden and could be replaced or eliminated without affecting either the story or its message. It is not people that Koestler develops in his novels but ideas. His discussion of the plight of the slaves, for example, is designed more to highlight the revolutionary ideology of Spartacus than to elicit sympathy for the slaves as such.[1] What Koestler takes for granted is that ideas, however much they may be intertwined with their historical and material environment, have an autonomy of their own and logical consequences independent of both.

Insofar as anything that could be called a proletariat is concerned, *The Gladiators* is the only novel by Koestler where they play any role whatever. For Koestler the masses represent inarticulate feelings that cannot find easy expression. But for most of Koestler's work there are no submerged or inexpressible ideas. His ideas are always dramatic, stark, and fairly bursting into voice. The persons chosen in his fiction to convey those ideas therefore tend to be articulate intellectual spokesmen who are never at a loss for words or the proper framework within which to express them.

The cosmological setting for *The Gladiators* is larger than its historical symbolism. On the grand scale, it is a rebellion that eventually grows into a revolution not merely against the repressive order of the Roman Empire but also against the order of the human condition itself, as that condition has been created by someone else. As such, Koestler understands the thrust of modern revolutions at their theoretical core to be against God as the author of that condition. The political task of revolutionaries is to create an order and meaning out of the cosmic chaos in which they find themsevles. The symbol of that order, which is of necessity placed in the future, is a utopian vision in *The Gladiators* that is referred to as the Sun State. The tragedy of Spartacus is that to get from oppression to utopia he must follow what Koestler calls "the law of detours." That is, he must walk a crooked road in order to reach the pure and untainted end he sees before him in his mind's eye. The means of getting to that end must occupy all of his attention. The paradox and the tragedy is that it is the very crookedness of the road that effectively prevents him from ever reaching the imagined utopia. Perfection, Koestler is saying here, is of the intellect and not of the world. And because it is of the intellect only, theory and practice in politics cannot be truly joined together. A true revōlutionary praxis is an illusion.

The Gladiators is divided into four parts that chronicle the growth of the rebellion into revolution. Each of these parts forms a separate commentary on different aspects of the revolutionary dilemma. Taken together, they form the basis for most of Koestler's subsequent departures on the dilemma of ends and means. Although *The Gladiators* is not as well known as *Darkness at Noon*, it foreshadows the arguments of the latter novel and makes many of the same points from the opposite side of the yogi-commissar spectrum.

I *Rise*

Spartacus' revolt takes place in the Roman Empire at the beginning of its decadance. It is evident from the opening lines that the full depth of the empire's decadance and depravity is grasped only by the intellectuals. The reasons for the corruption and for possible cures are developed through a small cadre of intellectuals who speak for the inarticulate masses.

Fluvius the lawyer, a democratic spokesman for the downtrodden of Rome, gives the reader the first picture of life in Rome. The city has gone downhill because of the existence of the slaves themselves. Once the city was full of workers who produced wealth, but now wealth is imported into Rome, which simply consumes without producing. The indigenous population has been reduced to the status of beggars and thieves because they have no economic function in the consuming city. Rome's economy has ceased to grow, according to Fluvius, except by conquests that are now at a standstill. Hence the quality of even this miserable life in the city must contract. As substitutes for work, the rulers give the people circuses in the form of gladiator contests to the death. These contests are the ultimate degradation of man, but within them are contained the potential seeds for Rome's downfall.

Brutal though life in Rome is for most of its inhabitants, Koestler implicitly invites a comparison between the decadance of Rome and the modern world. The assumption by analogy is that things have not really changed all that much. The material and spiritual poverty of both eras have made them a time of revolution. But the revolutions are, as Fluvius hastens to add, "abortive revolutions."[2] None of the many revolutions have seriously shaken the foundations of the prevailing social and political institutions. Given the obvious corruption of the Roman polity, the question Fluvius asks is "why" have the revolutions failed. The answer he gives is the narrative of the rise and fall of the Sun State.

The first part of Koestler's argument in *The Gladiators* is dominated by Fluvius. It is a significant point that helps to set the tone for what follows. Fluvius is an intellectual and not a man of action in the strictly commissar sense of the word. It is partly because of this that he has failed to attract any widespread popular following. As he reflects on the failure of his appeal as a democratic leader, it does not seem that the failure can be due to any intellectual failing. The failure, he concludes, is with the masses themselves, who do not understand the laws of history; however miserable their lot, they love the circuses and despise the intellectuals. They are unable to establish any cause-effect link between their miserable lot and the necessity for revolution. Hence their occasional revolts are little more than bread riots. There is certainly no proletarian class consciousness that could form the basis for a revolutionary vanguard.

In the person of Fluvius, Koestler early fixes in the mind of the reader his notion that revolutionary ideologies begin as intellectual constructions and are not the result of impersonal historical forces. But the utter indifference and even the hostility of the poor toward Fluvius has no impact on his actions. He still feels a moral obligation to lead them into the new utopia of his mind, only it will have to be in spite of them and against them at times rather than because of them. Fluvius cannot link his abstract revolutionary ideas with a plan of action until the unexpected revolt of some seventy gladiators provides him with a vehicle to test his theories in practice.

The revolt of the gladiators is purely spontaneous. They are in rebellion against their immediate surroundings and are not yet revolutionaries in the commissar meaning of the term. Their revolt is against the polluted society around them, but they have not yet found anything to be pulled toward. The movement toward a utopia begins when they accidently discover that they have allies among the people as a whole. When they easily defeat a small band of local militia sent to suppress them, several of the survivors join their band. Afterwards, they roam the countryside together as an early version of Robin Hood. In their wanderings, other slaves run away from their masters and join them, and the tiny band grows into a force to be reckoned with. There is no mistaking the appeal the revolution has for the oppressed peoples, and one could argue from this that there is a proletarian quality about the novel. But the historical setting mitigates against this interpretation. The reader knows beforehand that Rome will not fall because of Spartacus. However much the reader may sympathize with the goals of the revolt, the question that remains uppermost in his mind is why the revolt ultimately fails to bring Rome down despite its obvious corruption.

In the development of the gladiator revolt into revolution, the decisive moment comes when Fluvius and other intellectuals join the movement. The intellectuals with their wealth of ideas provide the catalyst for the change. This is a subtle but important shift away from the sequence of events that Marx had described in *The Communist Manifesto*. For Marx, the intellectuals joined in revolution that was already in progress. But for Koestler it does not become a revolution, as distinguished from simple revolt, until the intellectuals begin to shape its form and function. At this point the form of the movement, as a party of the revolution, is a product of its function, the movement toward the Sun State. In Koestler's version, intellectuals create a revolution out of what would otherwise be simply a formless revolt.

As the intellectuals shape the revolt into a revolution, it becomes a movement not only against the political order of Rome, but against the entire cosmic order that stands behind the dilemmas of the human condition. All of the protagonists in the novel find themselves locked into conflict not only with each other but with a fate that is larger than all of them combined. It is their common enemy. The historical forces are not rational, as they were for Hegel's "cunning of reason," but are ignorant or neutral in the struggles that take place. The laws of history are not necessarily on the side of the revolutionaries. The notion of a deaf and dumb cosmos that is uncaring about the fate of man is a constant and recurring theme in Koestler's work.

After Fluvius, the most important intellectual who gives the movement its theoretical cast of mind is an Essene. Historically, the Essenes were one of the Jewish sects that practiced a primitive form of communism. Exactly how and when the Essene came to join the gladiators is not exactly clear. Apparently a slave at first, he quickly rose to a position of authority as "a man who can read." Most important is what he reads. As a Jew, he is steeped in the tradition of Jewish prophecy and sees Spartacus immediately as "the son of man" who is destined to bring an end to the rule of the wicked on earth.[3] He knows from his knowledge of the Old Testament that the secular world is governed by beasts and that it is the destiny of a messiah to end that rule. The old order is to be swept aside by the messiah as the new Jerusalem is to be built in its place. The revolution ordained by God is immanent, total, and apocalyptic in nature.

Although Spartacus resists seeing himself in such a role at first, the opportunity is finally too much for him to resist. The Essene assures him that it is not necessary that he be specifically named as the son of man. "It is the same with prophecies as with clothes," the Essene says, "There they hang in the tailor's shop, many men pass them, many a man they would fit. . . . What really matters is, that it suits fashion and period."[4] In the dichotomy of the yogi and the commissar, what Koestler is saying is that any man could, potentially at least, play either role. All one need do to become a commissar is make a given choice and accept the consequences. With the seed of the idea planted in Spartacus, he is on the road to his conversion experience; "Lots of flies seem to hum inside my head," he says.[5]

What the prophecy means to the Essene, and through him to

Spartacus, is that the kingdom of God on earth will be a communist kingdom. It is an egalitarial ideal born of the prophetic tradition from which he has come. As he looks about himself, he can see signs of a communistic social organization spontaneously springing up among the former slaves. All that need be done is to politically complete the process already begun. What the Essene first tells Spartacus at this point is that the revolution will be abortive unless it is transformed into the quest for perfection itself. The self-imposed task of the Essene is to convince Spartacus that his destiny and the intellectual's vision are one and the same.

There is a deliberate touch of tragic irony in the fact that the Essene should take Spartacus to be the realization of the messiah. Initially it would appear that Koestler is creating a fictional Christlike figure along the lines of a Melville or Dostoevsky. But upon closer examination it appears that what Koestler intends is subtly different. In order to dress Spartacus in the clothes of Old Testament prophecy he changes the interpretation of the prophetic tradition. A conventional understanding of the Old Testament prophetic tradition would say that the origin of the Word the prophet heralds is outside of himself and came from God. The prophecy of the Essene, however, and consequently the idea of prophecy as Koestler uses the term, is that of man cut off completely from God. The Essene describes his no longer relevant God: "He was good at things of the desert; he knew how to open springs in the rocks and how to make bread rain from the heavens. But he knew nothing of industry and agriculture . . . he was no luxuriant God, but was hard and just like the desert itself. Therefore, he scolds at modern life and gets lost in it."[6]

What Koestler is saying here is that the desert God of the Jews is no longer able or willing to insure the fulfillment of His own prophecies. Modern life is too much unlike that of Moses or Isaiah for the old God to be of any help. Yet there is a destiny even beyond this God that still beckons, and it is that destiny that now calls Spartacus to its fold.[7] The chief difference between prophecy as conceived by the Essene and more traditioal interpretations is that for the former men now have their fate in their own hands rather in those of a divinity. Whatever will henceforth happen to man in the modern world of agriculture and industry cannot be the will of an irrelevant God but rather the product of man's own will. Meaning and purpose in man's life are now to be built on the visions of intellectuals.

Prophecy as the Essene presents it still retains much of the formal structure of biblical prophecy. But its content is dramatically altered to fit its newer function of serving the revolutionary purpose. It is a secular prophecy, as befits a commissar. But even here there is a further twist in Koestler that gives it an unmistakable pessimism. From the perspective of the twentieth century, Koestler implies that Christiantiy has proven no more successful than Spartacus would have been had he succeeded in changing the dilemmas of the human condition. Although Spartacus had no possible way of knowing that the Christian's Messiah was only a few decades away, the reader cannot help but be aware of that fact. It is Koestler's way of saying that even if his characters had known of it, and if they could also have known of its ultimate failure two thousand years later, it would not have made any substantive difference for a revolutionary praxis. Things would still be the same. In Koestler's later sketch of Christ in *The Call-Girls* (1972), he makes this point even more emphatic. For man and Jesus alike, heaven is an illusion.

The prophetic call to which Spartacus responds is a purely intellectual construct in which it is possible to see the Essene as a fool or a deceiver or both. But that intellectual construct, hollow though it may be, embodies a truth of its own and cannot be resisted by a man thirsting for religious faith. Modern cities have produced their own versions of truth, and their followers, like Zarathustra, have proclaimed the death of the desert God and His truth along with Him. Modern prophecy thus is seen as in opposition to divine prophecy. Its emphasis is wholly on immanence rather than a tension between immanence and transcendence. It is the prophecy of the Sun State and not the city of God. In the transition process, Spartacus becomes the living god who assures, in his role as commissar, fulfillment within earthly time.

What is most significant in Koestler's treatment of the linkage between revolutionary movements and a reverse Christological symbolism is his recognition of the roots of the revolutionary tradition. As with Camus' *The Rebel*, he sees it as the ultimate secular revolt against the Christian world view. But unlike Camus, he does not see it as an exclusively anti-Christian revolt. It is in the nature of the dilemma to be applicable to any cultural setting. In the West this means opposition to the Judaic-Christian heritage, but in other cultures it would take different forms. In the twentieth century it borrows its symbolic expression from Marx, but that is partly accidental.

While Koestler is consciously aware of this religious symbolism in modern revolutionary ideologies, and in spite of his theoretical identification with the commissar rather than the yogi, he is uncomfortable with it. It is a point of ambiguity more than anything else. There is no indication in his writing that he regards such reversal of symbolism as a theoretical error. Such symbolic ordering of the dilemmas of the human condition are simply an inescapable part of the modern world of the commissar. Presumably one cannot be a commissar without accepting this gnostic world view. This frank acceptance of a gnostic element in revolutionary ideology is a part of the more generalized dilemma of ends and means.

II   *The Law of Detours*

The political dilemma of Spartacus' revolution is spelled out by Koestler in what he calls "the law of detours." It is the predicament of the commissar who would heed the yogi's advice on means over ends. It is an iron law of revolutions that whoever would set out on the road to utopia must be "ruthless for the sake of pity."[8] The true revolutionary must be prepared to allow nothing to stand in the way of the end sought. To deviate from that straight path to the goal, to allow the means to prevail over the end, would mean the downfall of the revolution. It is a harsh law, but a necessary one for human progress. The fate of the gladiator revolution is that it falls victim to that law, as it allows the means to prevail at certain crucial junctures in the course of the movement toward the end.

The Gladiators is the only one of Koestler's novels in which he expressly uses the term "law of detours" in connection with the dilemma of ends and means. The importance of it as a concept in his overall work, however, goes far beyond this single novel. Neither of his subsequent novels in the trilogy, *Darkness at Noon* and *Arrival and Departure,* can be fully understood without reference to it. It is the first step in his working out of the reasons why revolutions inevitably fail. The question he asks with this concept is what would happen to a revolution if the leader allowed means to dominate ends? It was a question of intense discussion in the 1930s in light of Stalin's purge trials. Is the party of the revolution destined only to take the shortest route to the end, or may it make diversions along the way and still arrive at the same end? The application of the law of detours, although not the law itself, is dependent upon the will of the leader. It is he who must make the choices of ends or means.

The practical importance of the law of detours is introduced when the slave army captures its first town. Before the fall of the town of Nola, runaway slaves had flocked to the banner of revolt. They were the primary source of recruits and intelligence for the movement. But with the capture of Nola, the pentup frustration of the oppressed slaves was vented and in the process the city was burned to the ground. The dead included both master and slave, the innocent along with the guilty. It marked a decisive turning point for the movement, which up till that time had known nothing but an unbroken string of victories. But after the wanton carnage at Nola, the slaves no longer flocked to the movement, although it continued to attract its share of intellectuals. In fact, for the first time, slaves now began to side with their masters and against Spartacus. As for the army of the revolution, "they had come down from Mt. Vesuvius to found the Sun State, had sown fire and reaped ashes."[9]

How did the sacking of Nola fit into the law of detours? According to the law, what Spartacus should have done was to punish those within the movement who had allowed their emotions to destroy the purity of the revolution. Instead he hesitated and allowed them to go free. When the reader then asks why Rome did not fall of its own corruption, Koestler's answer lies in the inability or unwillingness of the revolutionary leader to apply in fact the theoretical insights of the revolutionary ideology. It is a failure of the applicability of theory to practice. What Spartacus does is allow humanitarian means to corrupt utopian ends.

The law of detours emerges in *The Gladiators* as an objective law of politics as valid as the law of gravity in physics. It cannot be violated except at the cost of failure. It is a law, however, that unlike its counterpart in physics requires theoretical articulation to be understood in practice. The slaves, for example, cannot really see the end and are only concerned with the present in politics. In Marxist terms, the proletariat lacks the revolutionary consciousness necessary to consummate the movement. The law of detours must therefore be promulgated to be known and that is the task of the intellectuals. These intellectuals must rationalize the law of detours to their followers in much the same way other intellectuals had rationalized Stalin during the 1930s. They must explain the necessity for corrupt means in the attainment of uncorrupted ends.

Koestler presents his law of detours in *The Gladiators* in a fragmentary form. In this first novel it is as if he is groping for a more systematic way of expressing the ends-means dilemma he later found in the yogi-commissar continuum. The thematic touchstone for this groping in *The Gladiators* is the role of prophecy in the law of detours. When the disappearance of God as the ordering force in human affairs, the commissar then takes His place. But because the commissar is himself the imperfect creation of that now defunct God, he is cursed by his own limitations. What ties these fragments together in the novel is the dilemma of an imperfect man, striving toward self-perfection, caught between the extremes of ends and means. The Essene frankly says it is the fault of God reflected in an imperfectly created human species:

God created the world in five days, and he was in too much of a hurry. Many things went wrong in all this hurry, and when he arrived at the making of man on the sixth day, he was tired and irritable perhaps, and burdened with many curses. But the worst curse of all is that he must tread the evil road for the sake of the good and right, that he must make detours and walk crookedly so that he may reach the straight goal.[10]

When this statement is combined with the assertion that the God of the desert is no longer present, the reader must interpret this curse of the law of detours to have been placed there by either an impotent God who can no longer lift it or a vengeful God who is perhaps Satanic. In *The Age of Longing,* Koestler calls the desert God of the Jews "insane." The commissar thus becomes a sort of Promethian figure in his rebellion against his inescapable dilemma. But it is a wholly futile gesture. Prometheus was punished by the gods for his act of defiance. But the commissar's gesture is met by nothing more than a cosmic abyss of dumb nothingness.

Since morality can no longer be defined in terms of the law of God, revolutionary ethics come to be the ethics of men who act the part of gods. This gives to the law of detours an unmistakenly Machiavellian undertone that surfaces both in the theory and practice of revolutions. The intellectuals argue, for example, that the revolution cannot be unjust by definition since it began as a revolt against injustice. Whatever Spartacus does to further the revolution's ends must be understood as just in the larger sense of the word, of the ends justifying the means. A distinction then comes to be made on what they call the "little truths," such as the destruction of Nola, and the "big truth," which is the construction of the Sun State in the future. In a revolution, the latter takes precedence over the former.

But Koestler does not allow the issue to rest comfortably here. The end can still be thwarted by the intrusion of these little truths. Which means support the "big truth" and which do not? What if the Sun State is merely an illusion, as it is in Koestler's novel? Then which acts are big truths and which are little truths? By the end of the novel, the conclusion seems to be that it is the destruction of towns that are in reality the big truths. What is not entirely clear, however, is whether or not this is the truth Koestler wanted to say or whether it is the truth he could not help but say. Honesty with himself is one of Koestler's principle hallmarks, and he has never hesitated to say things that he thought were true even if he wished they were not. Whatever the case, there is a tension in Koestler's many works between the big and little truths of theory and practice that appears over and over again.

It is one of the evils of the law of detours that it works a corrupting influence not only on the course of the revolution but on the souls of the revolutionaries themselves. As Spartacus comes increasingly under the sway of the Essene and other intellectuals, their theories eventually become a living part of his own actions. Theory and practice are united in his person. He is their word made flesh. His conscious actions are then directed toward molding himself into the idealized version of a revolutionary leader—the commissar. The change in his personality as a result was duly noted by Fluvius, who understood the change better than Spartacus. "Spartacus' development, then soon made him rise above the level of his companions, and made him realize that the latter acted like blind men or ignorant beasts who must be watched and forcably guided upon the right road. . . . He will have to make detours whose point is lost on others; for he alone can see, while they are blind."[11] Following the law of detours transforms Spartacus' outlook from one of warmth and respect for his followers to a distain for them. For the revolution, this represents a gain, as it is a loss for Spartacus personally. Now that he sees the ends of the revolution more clearly, he can unite theory and practice more effectively into his own person. Hereafter, to judge his actions aright, it will be necessary to judge them exclusively from the perspective of the law of detours and not the Ten Commandments. In effect, Spartacus becomes a law unto himself. The political tragedy for Koestler is that the nobelest intentions of human striving are turned around into the most dangerous results.

III   *The Sun State*

In *The Gladiators* version of history, Spartacus does briefly achieve a measure of success in the temporary creation of the Sun State. This was done by coming to terms with the other Italian cities that were willing to leave the ex-slaves alone while they conducted their experiment in utopia. In the context of the political arguments of the

1930s, this appears to have been a thinly disguised reference to the argument of "socialism in one country" that Stalin advocated against the world revolution of Trotsky. But the Sun State is Russia as it would have been without Stalin at the head. It is the best the Bolshevik Revolution could have hoped for with someone else at its topmost position.

The organization of the Sun State suggests what Koestler seems to have considered as the most desirable features of Communism. It is the way it should have worked. Like the Soviet Union in the twentieth century, the Sun State by its own barbarisms has cut itself off from growth by outside recruitment. The result is that the gladiator army is thrown back on its own resources. And the limited nature of those resources means sacrificing some of its most cherished ideals. It meant making peace with corrupt neighbors and returning runaway slaves to their masters. It meant that there would be no more proselytizing among the slaves of the outside cities. Hence it came to be that the Sun State was erected on a theoretical crime—the denial of the notion of universal justice for everyone. The narrow survival of the particular, the emphasis on means, was sacrificed to necessity. Although Spartacus could justify these actions by reference to the now infinitely plastic law of detours as it had developed in his mind, these were the actions that sowed the seeds for the final collapse of the Sun State.

What is perhaps most striking in Koestler's portrayal of the Sun State is the discrepancy between the real and the ideal. While it is obvious to the reader and the slaves as well that somehow practice does not match theory, there is no inclination by the slaves to leave. While it is not exactly what they wanted, it is still far better than anything else they have ever known. The actual physical construction of the Sun State satisfies their immediate goals. But the austere nature of its life after completion deadens their revolutionary spirit. The long-run goals, the utopian ends, were sacrificed to a present that could be understood by the masses.

While the city is under construction, Fluvius muses over the changes in the revolution since its inception. In retrospect it seems that it was the striving for utopia and not its impossible realization that was important. No political reality could ever measure up to the fantastic dreams of utopia that every man carried in his breast. With that, a terrible thought occured to him—what if justice were no more than an illusion and utopias merely a phantom of the mind's eye? "All these sufferings, all these turbid detours which it was said one had to take for the sake of the goal—were they perhaps not means to an end at all, were they the law of history itself; and the goal only human fancy—without any reality to back it up?"[12]

One of the reasons why revolutions are doomed from the beginning, according to Koestler, is that the idea of freedom is an emotion built on expectations and not a rational possibility. When the reality, which is a form of reason, is made manifest, the experience of a fall is all the greater because of the dreams that preceeded it. It would be better, Fluvius thinks, if men did not think so much about their condition. Echoing the sentiments of Rousseau, a thinking man is a depraved creature. The contradictions of life are too much for the ordinary person to bear. For intellectuals such as himself, knowledge of the cosmic void is maddening, but for the masses it would mean chaos. The illusion of utopian ends prophesied by the revolutionary party, therefore, can only be maintained by an iron discipline.

What is missing from Spartacus' leadership, however, is just that iron discipline. He is never able to bridge the gap between his vision of the end and its comprehension by his followers. "The old chasm between leader and common people has opened again," one of the ex-slaves remarks.[13] Unable to comprehend the logic behind his moves, Crixus, his second-in-command, leads a portion of disgruntled gladiators out of the Sun State to plunder one of the cities with which they have a treaty. The inability of Spartacus to reconcile theory and practice as the followers experience it in their daily lives leads to the downfall of the experiment. The law of detours keeps them chained to their own meager resources when there were riches in other cities for the taking. "What kind of crazy law was this which enjoined them to ever waxing privation and barred the logical way out of their present want."[14]

It has been the articulation of a vague longing for perfection that had originally transformed the gladiator revolt into a genuine revolution. But when the real did not match the ideal, the bitterness over the gap between them was directed toward an outside world that was held responsible for the failure of the revolution. If the Sun State could not raise itself to a higher level, then it would self-destruct and in the process bring its neighbors down to its level. The end of the dream of perfection came for Fluvius when the Sun State was indistinguishable in its acts from every other city. By "relapsing into ferocity and wolf's countenance of yore they destroyed the fundamentals on which their city rested, and no one was able to stay her decline and fall after this."[15]

When Crixus led his followers out of the Sun City in defiance of Spartacus, it was the beginning of the end. Spartacus saw that his actions would destroy more than just a nearby city. It would also break up the intricate system of treaties and alliances that enabled the Sun State to survive in peace. What Spartacus should have done at this point, as Koestler makes clear, was to have killed Crixus for trying to follow a different road to utopia. But instead, he allows his friendship for Crixus to interfere and again allows the means to prevail over the end. It was the last time Spartacus would have a choice of action in the law of detours.

Lest the reader get the impression that things might have turned out differently had the end prevailed over the means, had Crixus for example disposed of Spartacus, at the end of the novel Crixus says with a shrug, "It wouldn't have made any difference."[16] The inherent tragedy of the law of detours is that in the final analysis it does not really matter whether the leader and his revolution follow it or not—he is doomed to failure in either case.

IV *Decline*

The final section of *The Gladiators* is the shortest of the four parts. Since the reader knows from the opening pages that the revolution will ultimately fail, the fall itself is less significant than the reasons for it. The reasons are bound up with the implications of the law of detours. After the failure, a deep-seated pessimism hangs over the remainder of the novel. As Spartacus leads what now remains of his army out of the Sun State in aimless wanderings about Italy until his final defeat, he knows for the first time what a few intellectuals had dimly realized for some time—that the idea of a utopian polity is an illusion. But it is an illusion that still nourishes the spirit of the masses, and hence it is the duty of Spartacus to maintain it and feed its appetite. The notion that perfection is a chimera is a theme in all of Koestler's writing from *The Gladiators* till *The Call-Girls* over thirty years later.

If corruption seems to prevail over purity, it is not a complete victory. Just as there will always be a Rome, so too there will always be revolts against it. In the end, Spartacus is destroyed not by the military might of Rome but paradoxically by the roots of its corruption—capitalism in the person of Marcus Crassus. Crassus is the one person who can defeat Spartacus, because he alone knows the real power of money. "Money is not the means to profit and pleasure, but the means to power."[17] Having made that discovery early in life, he soon mastered the principles of economic and political power in Rome. He knew the days of the empire were numbered, but he also knew they would last out his lifetime.

Among the many adversaries of Sparticus, only Crassus was aware of the law of detours, since it governed his actions as well. Curiously, in these acts, he is more of an ideal commissar type than is Spartacus himself. He belives that ends and ends alone count. He had more in common with the brutality of Crixus' philosophy of "Eat or be eaten." In the end Spartacus recognized the similiarity between the two men and now recalls to himself that "Crixus had always been right in the end."[18] Belatedly he saw the primacy of ends.

Finally his army is defeated, and Spartacus along with the survivors are crucified along the Appian Way. The similarity here between the demise of Spartacus and that of Jesus a century later is not lost on Koestler. In his 1965 postscript to the Danube Edition he makes it clear that the comparison is deliberate. Specifically he says that he intended the ideas of Spartacus to be compared with the Sermon on the Mount.[19] Both, he says, were total failures as plans to establish justice here and now. In both cases, a polluted society crucified the leaders of a new and better social order. The great question for Koestler, however, is not merely a comparison of the two movements, but why they failed. For this question there can be no wholly satisfactory answer. Presumably the law of detours is as applicable to Spartacus as to Christ. No movement that hopes seriously to change the nature of the human condition can place all of its attention on either ends or means.

But despite his criticism of the revolution's emphasis of ends over means, Koestler still does not side with a ethic of means. At the end of *The Gladiators*, Koestler expresses his attitude on this point through the figure of Nicos, an old man from the gladiator school where the revolt first began. In the school Nicos had been like a father to Spartacus, but he had left the movement when its purity had been compromised at Nola. He represents the lost purity of the quest for utopia. He returns to the slave army at the very hour of its defeat because it has been purified once more by the spectacle of failure. Addressing Spartacus, he says, "Your way was not my way, but your end is my end."[20] Perfection, he goes on to say, is not a thing of this world, and because of it, all actions are wicked. But there can be a reason for some wickedness and not for others.

At this point Nicos then turns the ethics proclaimed in the Sermon on the Mount into their opposite. The Son of Man climbs to heaven to fight with an angel instead of descending into hell to fight with the Prince of Darkness. In the ethics of Nicos, the meek neither inherit the earth nor do they turn the other cheek. His speech is a gnostic reversal of the passages in Matthew with the opposite symbolism entirely. But it is a reversal of Christian ethics made necessary by the logic of ends and means, whereby man is caught between appalling alternatives and the God of the desert has disappeared altogether. "Blessed are those who take the sword in their hands to end the power of the Beasts; those who build towers of stone to gain the clouds, who climb the ladder to fight with an angel; for they are the true Sons of man."[21]

CHAPTER 4

Darkness at Noon

*D*arkness at Noon has been rightly recognized, both at the time of its original publication in 1941 and ever since, as one of the truly powerful works of twentieth century political literature. The passage of time has not in the least diminished its appeal. If anything, the novel has grown in stature because of the truth of its portrait of the ideological basis of totalitarian movements. The powerful combination of logic and passion make it a compelling masterpiece.

The central theme of *Darkness at Noon* is an exploration of the other side of the revolutionary dilemma discussed in *The Gladiators*—how and why revolutions fail when the end comes to dominate the means. Unlike the remote historical setting for *The Gladiators*, however, Koestler chose his own contemporary experience with the Russian Revolution and Communism as the basis for his novel. It reflects the fundamental tension in his own mind between thought and action and between ends and means. It must be understood that while he regards the revolution of the commissar as a failure, it does not follow that he regards the ethics of his opposite to be preferable. When a crucial decision must be made between the two, Koestler reluctantly casts his lot with the commissar. His critique of the commissar must therefore be viewed in this light.

Because *Darkness at Noon* is the best known and most influential of Koestler's work it is also the most controversial and has provoked the greatest response, both favorable and unfavorable. An adequate discussion of the novel will therefore have to take into account both aspects—the argument of the novel itself, as well as the reaction to it. This chapter will focus on the novel and the final chapter will consider some of the controversy it has spawned.

I *The Structure of the Novel*

The setting for *Darkness at Noon* is dramatically different from that of *The Gladiators*. Rather than a remote historical background, it is set in the bureaucratic underworld of a modern revolutionary state. It is the world of the commissar made politically manifest. The question raised is still the same as in the first novel: why do revolutions fail? The answer still turns on the issue of ends and means, but here the revolution fails because the vision of the end is allowed to over-shadow the means to that end. Could Spartacus' revolution have succeeded had he not followed the law of detours? Koestler's answer is "No."

The bureaucratic setting is Russia during the infamous Purge Trials of the 1930s. To much of the outside world, the purge of the old Bolsheviks was inexplicable, but to Koestler it reflected the inner logic of the revolutionary movement at its deepest level. What his novel did was to give to the trials a rational basis in the context of Marxist theory and practice that shocked and horrified its readers. Indeed, it is the very rationalism of the revolutionary terror that remains the true horror of *Darkness at Noon*. If the terror were irrational it would not be lacking in raw power, but would perhaps leave the impression that it could be tamed by reason. In the account by Koestler, however, the consequences of revolutionary logic may be deplored but the end result in no way alters the structure of its rationale. Who wills the end wills the means, Koestler says, and if you accept the commissar's vision of the end you cannot rationally refuse his means.

In *Darkness at Noon*, the reader's attention is directed toward the psychology of a single individual rather than the broad sweep of history that prevailed in *The Gladiators*. The effect of the change is to focus Koestler's points more sharply. But in the person of that single individual, Commissar Rubashov, the whole universe of revolutio-nary symbolism and theory is concentrated. His intellectual biog-raphy is the story of the revolution. In him all of the contradictions and consistancies of the ends-means dilemma find a home. In contrast with *The Gladiators*, there is very little physical action to distract attention from the theoretical argument.

The physical action of the novel is slight. It consists of the arrest, interrogation, trial, and execution of one Commissar Rubashov dur-ing the Moscow Purge Trials. Since the final fate of Rubashov is scarcely in doubt from the opening pages, the full attention of the reader is directed toward the reasons behind Rubashov's personal story rather than the fate of the particular individual. Furthermore, given the obvious though unstated reference to the Moscow trials, even the final confession itself can be surmised. All of this helps to make the theoretical logic of the outcome all the more fascinating. What the reader wants to know is "why" so many of the old guard freely confessed to crimes they never in fact committed. What Koestler supplies is the reason.

Because the rationale behind the confessions is the central theme, the most crucial aspects of the work deal with the interrogations of Rubashov. It is here that the ideological logic of the revolution is worked out. The interrogations are by two other commissars, Ivanov and Gletkin. Symbolically they do not represent different persons so much as Rubashov's own alter ego at different stages of ideological development. They are, therefore, always throwing back on him his own arguments, his own thoughts. The interrogations are thus more in the nature of a series of arguments Rubashov has with himself. There is no indication that Ivanov and Gletkin are other than different phases of Rubashov's own argument.

These modern commissars are the natural heirs of Spartacus but have learned the lesson of his mistakes. They have the same vision of a utopian end but are determined to keep it in view and not be sidetracked by the law of detours. It would be an anachronism for Koestler to have placed a modern revolutionary in a context such as that of Spartacus. The modern commissar is a theorist of ends, not means. The failure of modern revolutions, as distinguished from ancient ones, must be understood as failures of ends-dominated theories.

II *Who is Rubashov?*

The person of Rubashov poses one of the most difficult problems in any interpretation of *Darkness at Noon*. This is because he is both a symbolic figure and one whom Koestler intends to be interpreted literally. Koestler assembled Rubashov as a composite protrait of several acquaintances whom he knew personally and a number of old Bolsheviks whom he did not know on a firsthand basis. It is important to keep these twin aspects of Rubashov separate since the inability to do so has led to a number of misinterpretations.

Closely tied to the problem of *who* Rubashov represents is *what* he is in the novel. Literally, he is one of the last of the original revolutionaires who had made the revolution in his mind long before it had become an historical fact. As such, he is also one of the few to know from personal knowledge that a shadow has fallen between the dream and the reality of the revolution. Partly for this knowledge, perhaps even exclusively because of it, he is to be liquidated by No. 1, a euphemism Koestler reserves for Stalin. But while the reasons for liquidation are obscure, the rationale behind the public trial is not. He has been selected for an open, public trial precisely because he knows the ethics of the dream-end. He is a true believer. Were he not a true believer he could never be trusted to confess publically and would instead be unceremoniously murdered in private. Only the most trustworthy could be counted upon to play their assigned role as scapegoat for the regime in public and of their own free will. Above all, there must be no doubt by the party that he might suddenly recant his confession in public and thereby cast suspicion on the revolutionary purity of the party itself.

For Rubashov, the reason of the party is the source both of his greatest strength and of his fatal weakness. His rationalism is of a highly abstract order. His arguments on ends and means are cast in a purely theoretical foremat, and he has difficulty making the transition from theory to practice, even though the memory of that practice is the source of his own doubts. The practices of the revolution are constantly in the background, but only in the background. The working assumption of all the commissars is that it is ideas that are ultimate reality and the tangible fruits of those ideas are trivial by comparison. What follows, therefore, in Koestler's analysis is the testing of reason itself in pursuit of the revolutionary ideal.

In the literal interpretation of Rubashov, he is portrayed not as a real person, but a composite of real persons. In his physical appearance and biographical background, he bears a striking resemblance to Trotsky and Bukharin, respectively. While this has led many critics to see in Rubashov a fictional version of Bukharin in particular and to evaluate *Darkness at Noon* in terms of the literal congruity between the two, this similarity has too often been overdrawn. While Rubashov is intended by Koestler to be taken literally, there is more to it than that alone. Rubashov is a synthesis of persons, no doubt with some of Koestler's own personality thrown in for good measure. Physical similarities with actual persons, or the lack thereof, in no way destroys Koestler's argument. It is true enough to note that there may never have been a single victim in all the Purge Trials who embodies all of Rubashov's physical and mental traits. But the inability to find an exact historical counterpart cannot be taken as a serious rebuttal to the fictional Rubashov. Such criticisms would be more valid if Koestler had not intended Rubashov to posess a symbolic quality more important than the literal one.

At the symbolic level, Rubashov is more than merely a composite figure pasted together by an imaginative writer. First of all, it must be recalled that Koestler is chiefly concerned with ideas rather than with persons as such. His interest is in the logical consequences of theoretical notions. These ideas cannot be separated from the persons who hold to them, but neither does Koestler intend that the reader's attention should become overly absorbed in the individual to the exclusion of the idea. Rubashov's realism is not derived exclusively from a physical and/or biographical similarity to any actual person. It is also derived from the truth of the ideas he argues and how they shape his behavior during the interrogations and after. What Koestler is saying is that if the logic of the commissar is carried to its final conclusion, a Rubashov will be the result—and that there are individuals prepared to follow the commissar logic, even at the sacrifice of their own lives. What Rubashov believes and argues is what any true Communist would have to believe and argue in order to accept and justify the Moscow trials at their face value.

Symbolically, then, Rubashov is the embodiment of the idea of the perfect commissar. He is the modern materialistic rationalist stripped down to his political essence. In this symbolic construction of Rubashov, there is no doubt that Koestler has left himself open to certain telling criticisms. For example, the intense intellectualization of Rubashov's motives robs them of the more human elements of personality. As a fictional character, he is a person the reader can look at with sympathy or horror but seldom with a strong sense of personal identification. In part this is a result of Koestler's own proclivities as a writer. He is a master of description for pure ideas, but decidedly weaker in relating actions or emotions. Actions and emotions are distractions in Koestler's work, and it is a strength of Rubashov, as well as his weakness, that he is reduced to almost pure thought.

For the revolutionary personality, which Koestler has described as pure action-oriented, Rubashov's exclusive preoccupation with theory may seem incongruous. It may seem less so if two points are kept in mind. First, the yogi-commmissar spectrum was conceived as an attempt to rationally interpret what would otherwise be irrational. When Rubashov argues the commissar's position, it is for the purpose of theoretical clarification and not action-oriented demonstration. Secondly, the fact that forces Rubashov into a position of pure thought is his imprisonment. Unable to act politically, he has little alternative but to think. In this inability to act, Koestler is able to dramatize the theoretical aspects of revolution more clearly than he did with *The Gladiators*. The modern split between theory and practice is more intensified. It is not that Rubashov does not have an active side. The reader is constantly reminded of Rubashov's past actions in behalf of the party through a series of flashbacks. But these are always in the context of highlighting the sharp contrasts between idealized theory and a practice that is all too real. It is one of the basic features of *Darkness at Noon* that Koestler wants to put as much distance between theory and practice as the nature of the problem will permit in order to focus on the theoretical side.

Because the focus of the novel is on ideas, the truth of Koestler's work is very much dependent on the truth of the theoretical dilemma described. To understand Rubashov as Koestler intended him to be understood means that the theoretical symbolism must be preeminent over the literal representation.

At the symbolic level of interpretation, Rubashov is a split-personality. On the one hand he is the prototype commissar. But in addition, he is also representative of a type of secularized Christological symbolism. The Christ like features of Rubashov build throughout the novel in a variety of subtle ways until they reach a crescendo in the closing pages. This symbolism is, as has been noted, an extension of the same sort found in *The Gladiators*, but it is handled much more deftly in Rubashov than with Spartacus. The Purge Trials take on certain qualities of the trial and execution of Christ, but without the resurrection. But the trials in both cases can only be understood from the perspective of the totally dedicated individual—in this case the secularized revolutionary saint. Only a person with Rubashov's revolutionary insight into the higher truth of the will of the party would be expected to see the logic in the confession.

Rubashov represents the modern perversion of reason, but it remains a form of reason nonetheles. It is as a rationalist of the materialist mold that he is led to "think his thoughts through to their logical conclusion." Physical torture would only serve to divert attention away from the ideas of the movement. The confession to crimes that he never committed is not intended to cast Rubashov outside the revolution, but just the opposite. Confession is the only way that he can return to the fold. The confession serves to reunite the victim with the executioner in the common purpose of serving the revolution. Shortly after his arrest, Rubashov asked Ivanov, "Did I arrest you or did you arrest me?" There is more than just irony involved here. Their two roles could quite easily be reversed. So long as Rubashov either does not or cannot disassociate himself from the revolution he has, for all practical purposes, sanctioned his own arrest.[1] Since his personal life and the life of the revolution are inseparable, to deny the right of Ivanov to arrest and interrogate him would mean to deny the justice of the revolution and of his own life and actions as a part of it.

Had Rubashov confessed for reasons of physical torture, Koestler's novel might have more closely resembled Orwell's nightmare *Nineteen Eighty-Four*. It might have been easier to understand the trials in one sense if the confessions were forceably extracted, but the revolutionary unity of theory and practice would have been obscured. The freely given confession points toward an entirely different order of ideas in the service of revolution than does a tortured one. Although Rubashov presents the reader with the revolution in terms of almost pure reason, Koestler does not lose sight of the close relationship between the theory and practice of the revolutionary tradition. Here we can also see more clearly why Rubashov is not the "typical" victim of the trials but rather the "atypical" victim; the dilemma of ends and means for intellectual revolutionaries could not be explored otherwise. The final confession is necessary in order to keep the theoretical question clearly in view. Rubashov is a martyred saint of the revolution, not just another faceless nonentity. He is a faithful servant of the new god, who follows the laws, the reasons, the acts of the movement to their final and inevitable end. Ivanov, the first interrogator, knows instinctively that Rubashov is not really an outsider: "We both grew up in the same tradition and have on these matters the same conception. . . . Put yourself in my place—after all, our positions might equally be reversed."[2]

Ivanov knows that Rubashov will confess because of the logic of the party's, position, not by torture. He tells Gletkin, "When he has thought everything out to its logical conclusion he will capitulate . . . it won't be out of cowardice, but by logic."[3] This is one of the most crucial points in the novel about Rubashov and the confession. Unless it is understood that Rubashov confesses for reasons of logic and not fear, the point Koestler is making will be lost. Later, when Gletkin kills Ivanov and takes over supervision of the interrogation, he thinks that it is his brutal methods that finally breakdown Rubashov's willpower. But that is a by-product of his own theoretical illiteracy and action-oriented character. Rubashov knows that he confessed because of the logic of Gletkin's position and not because of its brute force. It is explicitly described as a "last service to the Party" and does not have a great deal in common with Winston's confession, for example, in *Nineteen Eighty-Four*. The terror in *Darkness at Noon* is not the physical terror of Orwell, but rather is the terrible logic of an idea—the idea that the end will justify the means. Ultimately it is not the party that destroys Rubashov, except in the physical sense. His real destruction is as much symbolic as literal and comes from his own hand as he lives out his idealized, theoretical life in a polluted world. His destruction follows the attempt to weld an abstract image of perfection together with a real and imperfect man. In the process, both are destroyed. It is reflective of the tragedy of the modern world in Koestler's eyes that this is so.

III   *The Interrogations*

The interrogation of Rubashov first by Ivanov and then by Gletkin takes place in three separate and distinct phases. Each phase has a symbolism and meaning of its own even as they are tied together in a single flow of reasoning. The three persons of the novel, Rubashov, Ivanov, and Gletkin, may be said to represent respectively the party past, the party present, and the party future. As the interrogators question Rubashov, it can be seen as arguments of the past attempting to come to grips with arguments of the present and future. All of these phases are crucial links in the chain of causality that begins with the past and progresses to the logical culmination. In this process, past, present, and future are separable for analytic purposes only and not in logic, as each phase is implicit in the other. Gletkin thus is not only a perfect commissar of the future, he is also implicitly what Rubashov already is as potential.

The three figures of the novel that surround the interrogation should be seen as a single piece. They are different but related aspects of the dilemma of ends and means. In this, Rubashov is presented at first as one who has lost faith in the revolution of the present because it does not seem to accord with his original dreams. The physical terror that has come with the revolution was not what he and his fellow theorists intended. But could the end in Gletkin have been avoided? Having willed the end, could he avoid willing the means? The answer is already suggested by the structure of the interrogation, but is incomplete until Rubashov thinks his thoughts through to the end. He knows at the outset that the present difficulty is a result of having abandoned morality as means: "As we have thrown overboard all conventions and rules of cricket-morality, our whole guiding principle is that of consequent logic. We are under the terrible compulsion to follow our thoughts down to its final consequence and act in accordance with it. We are sailing without ethical ballast."[4]

Rubashov's shaken faith in the revolution ought not to detain the reader for long. He has committed his life to the proposition that the end will justify the means, and though his appearance of doubt is real enough, it is primarily a literary device Koestler uses to begin his train of thought. The subsequent development of the logic of the dilemma is the process by which apologists for the purges also overcame their doubts. Rubashov's doubts are not merely his alone, but also those of an entire generation of Western intellectual revolutionaries.

Although Rubashov has separated ends from means in his mind, the question of means continually intrudes into his otherwise rational calculation of ends. It is an unwanted intrusion, lacking in reason, but it will not go away. It is part of what he dubs the "grammatical fiction," the fact of an unexpected discovery of conscience. While ends and means can be kept analytically separate, they cannot be kept practically separate. Although in his essay "The Yogi and the Commissar," Koestler maintained that pure thought and pure action were at opposite poles, few of his literary creations have ever been able to keep the two totally apart.

In the interrogation, Ivanov and Gletkin may also be seen as figures who move closer and closer to the ideal commissar as pure, unreflective action. They are Rubashov's alter ego whose task it is to mold him into the perfect commissar. What happens as a result is that a rift is opened up in his personality between his idealized self and his real self. It produces a definite neurosis in his personality. In turn, this neurosis in Rubashov is his personal link to the moral defect of the revolution. The neurotic revolutionary personality is born of the rupture between an idealized image of the self, capable of realization only in the party, and the real self that is full of doubts. His denial of his imperfect self corresponds with a denial of genuine morality as means. "Perhaps the heart of the evil lay there," he thought to himself, "Perhaps it did not suit mankind to sail without ballast."[5] But as the interrogation eventually leads him to accept the end of the revolution sailing without ballast, it must be said that he knowingly and willingly accepts the evil means that go with it.

IV   The Logic of the Confession
and the "Grammatical Fiction"

Darkness at Noon opens with a deliberate link between the Communist and Fascist revolutions. The link is not at the theoretical level, but at the practical level of means. In order to oppose the Fascists, the Communists have become just like them in practice. When the party comes to arrest Rubashov, he is asleep. As he awakens, he has difficulty deciding who it is that has come for him. Is he asleep and dreaming of being arrested in a Fascist country, or is he awake and actually being arrested in the country of the revolution? What follows until the end of the novel could have been duplicated with only a slight variation in a Fascist state. Furthermore, since neither Communism nor Stalin are ever mentioned by name, it is always relatively easy to substitute one regime for another in the double-edged symbolism. At the end, after he has been struck by one of the two fatal bullets in the back of the head, Rubashov looks up at a picture of No. 1 and is uncertain whether it is Hitler or Stalin he sees: "But whose color-print was hanging over his bed and looking at him? Was it No. 1 or was it the other—he with the ironic smile or he with the glassy gaze? . . . what insignia did the figure wear on the sleeves and shoulder-straps of its uniform—and in whose name did it raise the dark pistol barrel."[6]

This powerful symbolic effect of tying Communist terror to Fascist terror at the practical level is no doubt one of the principle reasons for the timelessness of the work. It is also Koestler's reminder to the reader that the dilemma of ends and means is not exclusively a Marxist problem. Furthermore, it must be understood that it is only at the practical level that Communism and Fascism appear to be the same. At the theoretical level, Fascism is unreflective evil whereas Marxism seeks to justify its deeds. Gletkin could be as Fascist, but Rubashov could never be one. Whether this is a difference that makes a difference is a question Koestler never pursued. He did raise the issue again briefly in *Arrival and Departure*, but he never developed the logic of it.

The logic of the confession does not turn on the objective guilt or innocence of Rubashov on the specific charges. The reader knows he is innocent in the usual meaning of the term. But of what, if anything, can he justly be considered guilty? Here it seems that Koestler intends the answer to depend upon the level in which such judgement is made. At the ideological level of party reasoning, he is guilty of counterrevolutionary heresy for harboring doubts about the revolution. At the personal level, Rubashov has the nagging feeling that he is indeed guilty of having used means to further the end of the revolution that are vaguely immoral, though he has no basis other than the end sought from which to decide moral questions. The knowledge that he has destroyed countless lives to further the goal of the revolution weighs heavily on a newly discovered conscience. There is a profound tension between these two poles of guilt in the eyes of the party and guilt in his own eyes. Rubashov finally resolves the tension by deciding in favor of the party, symbolizing the final triumph of ends over means. But the reader is left with an awareness that his real self is also guilty of sins of commission in means.

For the party there is only one crime—"to swerve from the course laid out: and only one punishment: death."[7] The party does not believe in or follow the law of detours. It does not argue that there may be separate roads to the same end or that some compromises along the way may be necessary. The party line "is sharply defined, like a narrow path in the mountains. The slightest false step, right or left, takes one down the precipice."[8] What matters to the party are not "subjective" motivations, but the logical consequence of ideas that are of their nature "objective." For the party it is sufficient that Rubashov has experienced a single twinge of doubt. If he no longer wills the end, he must will means that are destructive of that end. From a single fleeting doubt, the party can logically construct his intention to undermine the revolution.

The first interrogation by Ivanov brings out this point dramatically. The charges that he is an active agent of certain counterrevolutionary elements is patently false, at least in terms of overt actions. But when he admits to Ivanov that for some time he has harbored doubts about certain party actions, he is caught in an ideological web from which there is no escape. Ivanov confronts him with the logic of his doubts: "You now openly admit that for years you have had the conviction that we were ruining the Revolution; and in the same breath you deny that you belonged to the opposition. . . . Do you really expect me to believe that you sat watching us with your hands in your lap—while, according to your conviction, we led the country and Party to destruction."[9]

Ivanov could never have confronted Rubashov with this line of reasoning had not both agreed beforehand that actions logically follow thought and that the two are intrinsically in harmony. Rubashov knows this and agrees that Ivanov has reason on his side; "Logically you may be right," he says. What Rubashov refuses to link together at this point in the interrogation is the praxis between theory and practice. A confession will necessitate an acceptance of that cause-effect relationship. It will require an acceptance of his idealized self at the expense of his real self. This has suddenly become an important consideration for Rubashov, because in his jail cell he has, for the first time, discovered that he has two selves. He calls this new self, his conscience, the "grammatical fiction."

Rubashov's guilt at the practical level, the level where means are most important, is presented in the form of what Koestler calls this grammatical fiction.[10] It is a dimension of reality discovered in prison that is entirely unknown to the previous conception of the commissar's rationalism. It is an inner voice, an unwanted and wholly unexpected discovery of individual existence that is distinct from corporate existence in the party form of class consciousness.

It is in the nature of this grammatical fiction that it defends the individual against the collective conscienceness. Koestler raises this notion to the highest possible level of symbolism. In one form or another, it became the moral touchstone of most of his subsequent writing. It was the basis upon which he engaged in later battles against behaviorists, psychologists, materialist philosophies, and any other examples of modern thought that tend to deny this notion of the reality of the individual soul. As Koestler conceptualizes it, there is a strong hint of a Kantian sort of distinction that seems to be wholly compatible with the yogi-commissar continuum. It has, alternatively, been the basis of Koestler's humanism and his defense of political means while theoretically siding with the ethic of ends in politics.

Rubashov experiences this grammatical fiction as something that seems to have taken possession of him against his will. That it is an integral part of his personhood, however, there is no doubt. Contrary to all the rules of grammar, it persists in addressing him as "I" instead of "You," as his materialist philosophy would have it. It is a silent partner that speaks even when he does not want to listen and without any visible pretext for starting the conversation. Rubashov fights it, unsuccessfully because it is a reminder of the gap between the theory and practice of the revolution as he originally conceived it. It threatens to upset all of his previous notions about the mechanical nature of reason as it reminds him of the problem of means.

The party, of course, does not recognize the existence of a grammatical fiction. Implicitly, however, the party does recognize something of the sort as one of the major obstacles standing in the way of the confession. For the party, there is no "I" in their vocabulary, but only the plural "We." The Party of "We" is at war with the individual.[11] Ivanov sees the heresy of Rubashov's continual referal to the party as "You," implying that he has an existence apart from it. The interrogation and Rubashov's final confession represent a struggle to subordinate the "I" to the "We" and to return to the logic of ends over means.

The logic of the commissar eventually overwhelms the grammatical fiction. In part this is because Rubashov cannot reduce it to a rational thing and dissect it scientifically. The voice of conscience thus appears to be something outside of reason. Of all the things in his world, the grammatical fiction is the one uncaused effect. He cannot argue with it, as it claims an autonomy independent of reason alone.

At times this voice of conscience is cast symbolically as Rubashov's toothache. The toothache is a result of a Fascist beating. It comes and goes whenever his conscience ought to be bothering him during the interrogation. It is finally assuaged only at the end of the novel when he confesses. When the "I" disappears and only the "We" remains, the toothache and the grammatical fiction are no longer part of Rubashov's life. It is the end of the struggle between theory and practice.

The confession is built on the supression of the grammatical fiction, but it also involves the creation of an historical fiction—the idea of the progress of history. History is, as Koestler well knows, the god of revolution. He makes clear that this historicized world view is the product of Marxist thought. The party, as the inheritor of this tradition, knows nothing of conscience and toothaches. Scientific history knows only ends and the party as its prophet. As Rubashov recalls: "The Party is the embodiment of the revolutionary idea in history. History knows no scruples and no hesitation. Inert and unerring she flows toward her goal. . . .History knows her way. She makes no mistakes. He who has not absolute faith in History does not belong in the Party's ranks."[12]

History, like the commissar's ethic of ends, is morally neutral. When Rubashov puzzles over means, he has cast himself outside the stream of history as well as the party. The party is absolved of all sins, since it is merely the agent of the mechanistic god of a material universe. It is in the end impossible for Rubashov to hold either Gletkin or the party responsible even for his own death because they are merely the agents of the new god.

The final confession is Rubashov's "last service to the Party." At this point, the party needs villans as black as pitch and not heroes. Rubashov has his assigned part to play and can do no less than play it. There is a strong temptation to "die in silence," but that would be petty bourgeois morality. His subject guilt is real, in terms of the logic of both the party and himself. He "had followed every thought to its last conclusion and acted in accordance with it to the very end."[13] In confessing of his own free will, which the party has ironically denied, Rubashov is, as Koestler makes clear, the exception and not the rule among the victims of the purge. Most confessed because of torture, but "the best of them," meaning the saints of the revolution, did so as the "We" had its final triumph over the "I." They returned to the fold.

V   The Unity of Theory and Practice

Unlike the revolution of Spartacus, the new revolution has come to power and held on to it. But it was a predictable failure all the same. It too is founded on an illusion. There is no utopia ordained by history or any other god. The attempts to build utopias inevitably end in tragedy, but not always for the same reasons. Spartacus failed because he followed the law of detours; the Russian Revolution failed because it did not. For Koestler, there is no middle ground, and the would-be revolutionary cannot escape failure. The Moscow trials were not, therefore, an aberrition of Marxism, but its very essence: "[The commissars] dreamed of power with the object of abolishing power; of ruling over people to wean them from the habit of being ruled. All their thoughts became deeds and all their dreams were fulfilled."[14]

The difficulty with the modern notion of praxis in revolution is that it is tied to a notion of reason that has become demonic in its consequences. Ivanov confronts Rubashov with this fact during the first interrogation: "In the old days temptation was of a carnal nature. Now it takes the form of pure reason. The values change. I would like to write a Passion play in which God and the Devil dispute for the soul of Saint Rubashov."[15]

But reason is not on the same side as God. It is the ally of the revolutionary and the enemy of the desert God of the Jews. The reason of the commissar is the Promethian reason of Marx and loses none of its appeal or power by siding with evil:

Satan [is] . . . a fanatical devotee of logic. He reads Machiavelli, Ignatius of Loyola, Marx and Hegel; he is cold and unmerciful to mankind, out of a kind of mathematical mercifulness. He is damned always to do that which is most repugnant to him. . .to strip himself of every scruple in the name of a higher scrupulousness, and to challenge the hatred of mankind because of his love for it—as abstract and geometric love.[16]

Reason is thus not only on the side of Satan, but against means as well. In any debate over ends and means that is conducted according to logic and reason alone, the ends will always emerge triumphant. This is the true terror of the revolution to Koestler—its alliance with reason. It is why the grammatical fiction loses the debate with reason. It is Rubashov's inability to argue against Ivanov and Gletkin that eventually brings him back into the party's ranks voluntarily. The commissar wins the argument with the yogi. Conscience may occasionally triumph, but only at the cost of reason: *"Apage Satanas!* Comrade Rubashov prefers to become a martyr. The columnists of the liberal press, who hated him during his lifetime, will sanctify him after his death. He has discovered a conscience, and a conscience renders one as unfit for the revolution as a double chin. Conscience eats through the brain like a cancer."[17]

Ivanov does not silence Rubashov's conscience by logic alone, but he does defeat it. The arguments of the party are those of the future, whereas conscience belongs to the prehistoric past. Rubashov's doubts, representing the party past, cannot answer the party present in Ivanov and thus succumb to the party future in Gletkin. This future in Gletkin now appears to have been ordained from the beginning, and Rubashov can no more deny the logic of Gletkin than he could deny himself. During the last interrogation, conducted by Gletkin, Ivanov has already forged the link that joins Gletkin and Rubashov together like father and son. The unity of theory and practice in Marxist praxis is one more established in Rubashov's mind. In Gletkin, it is his future self that he confronts with the logical conclusion of his own arguments and his own reason.

Gletkin's interrogation is a more harsh one than that conducted by Ivanov, but that is because Gletkin is the "new man" of socialist consciousness. Gletkin believes that it is his methods that get Rubashov to confess, but the old commissar knows better. Gletkin is "a repellant creature, but he represents the new generation." He is a more pure commissar than Rubashov, "the generation which started to think after the flood. It has no traditions, and no memories to bind it to the old, vanished world. It was a generation born without an unbilical cord. . . . And yet it had right on its side."[18]

Compared to Gletkin, Rubashov, with his grammatical fiction, is described as an ape looking with ignorant scorn at the first man. Gletkin is "the barbarian of the new age which is now starting." But he is also the necessary first step along the evolutionary path toward the classless man of the future. He is Rubashov's ideological son and the rightful heir to the revolution. Though he is an unreflective individual, he was anticipated by the revolutionary theoreticians such as Rubashov. It is not in spite of his beastial qualities but because of them that he is now the right man in the right place at the right time to further the ends of the revolution. He has no scruples over ends and means—it is a nonexistant problem. As Rubashov prepares his final confession at the public trial, he thinks of Gletkin: "You don't understand the issue, but, did you understand, you would be useless to us."[19] The key here is that at the end Rubashov speaks of himself and Gletkin as "Us"—the triumph of the "We" over the "I."

VI   *The Religious Symbolism in Darkness at Noon*

In *Darkness at Noon,* the god of revolution is history. It is an amoral, perhaps even immoral, god that determines the form of rational and ethical behavior. Like all gods, it demands certain sacrifices. With the party sacrifice of Rubashov to the new god go the last traces of what the West had always understood as the concept of the soul—here portrayed as the grammatical fiction. Koestler makes Rubashov into a secularized saint of revolution, and he does so by contrasting it with a more orthodox saintliness in the biblical tradition. It is an extension of the same symbolism found in *The Gladiators.*

Rubashov's story, from arrest to execution, is so closely tied to a form of reverse Christian symbolism that to overlook it would result in a misreading of the novel. That symbolism begins with the arrest scene. As Rubashov is getting dressed, he looks down at his own feet and recalls a verse from his early childhood "which compared the feet of Christ to a white roebuck in a thornbush."[20] The attention of the reader is thus drawn at the outset to compare Rubashov with Christ. Unlike Christ, however, Rubashov is not portrayed as innocent in any sense. Like Christ, he is innocent of the crime alleged by his accusors, but he is guilty of other crimes in his conscience. Absolution from past sins comes when he submits to the new god that is explicitly opposed to the desert God of the Jews and hence to Christians as well.

Even Rubashov's most conspicuous traits and habits take on a decidedly religious connotation. The connection between his toothache and his conscience has already been mentioned; but in addition, his nervous habit of rubbing his glasses on his sleeve throughout the interrogation is described by Koestler as an act similar to "praying with a rosary."[21] This modest action is a symbolic and reflexive prayer that assuages his toothache—conscience whenever Ivanov and Gletkin are tempting him with a Santanic reason. At the end of the novel, as Gletkin is taking him out to his ignominious Calvary, he drops his glasses and is lost without them. This has a double significance. Not only is his physical vision lost, but his spiritual vision as well.

During his confession at the public trial, the daughter of an old comrade reads the account to her father. Alternately, the reader hears the confession of Rubashov and the old man's recollections of the Gospel passages where Christ is executed. The confession, however, is also different than Christ's condemnation. In the end, Rubashov suffers the same fate as Spartacus. The fate of the yogi turns out to be the same as that of the commissar. Christian principles are no more effective in Koestler's view than those of the commissar. The trial of Christ is the mirror image of the Moscow trials; everything is reversed, including the guilt of the two accused—yet the result is the same, the death of each, without changing the nature of the human condition. They are opposites in all respects save one. They are both failures. One is a failure of means over ends and the other is a failure of ends over means, but at the practical level this does not seem to matter much. For Rubashov the grave is the end; there is no resurrection. There is no heaven on earth or anywhere else for that matter. The religious symbolism in Koestler thus creates a mood of hopelessness and pessimism. It is a conscious reversal of Christian symbolism but a continuation of the same themes from *The Gladiators*.

CHAPTER 5

Between Past and Future

A RTHUR Koestler's third novel on the dilemma of revolutionary ethics was *Arrival and Departure*. Published in 1943, at the height of World War II, it is his most pessimistic work and yet shows a glimmer of optimism at the end that is a prominant feature of his writing. The novel represents his first attempt to consider if there is a way out of the dilemma posed by the yogi and the commissar—Is there a middle ground somewhere between the extremes? His answer is equivocal. Yes, there is a middle ground, but not for the political activist. The problem of *Arrival and Departure* is to explore the conflict between expediency and morality as reflected in an individual caught, not unlike Koestler himself, between the extremes. His message is that unless one can overcome personal hesitations involved in this agonizing choice, the result will be a paralysis of the will to act politically. One must chose one way or the other, as other alternatives are an illusion.

It is through the character of Peter Slavek that Koestler pursues his theme of an individual torn between expediency and morality. As an ex-party member, his situation is similar to that of Koestler himself. It helps to give to the novel a strong autobiographical flavor. For most of the novel, Peter is suspended between the yogi and the commissar, unable to chose which way to go. His inability to decide is symbolized in part by a physical paralysis that is entirely psychological. The structure of political choice then comes to turn on the dilemmas of choice as opposed to the refusal to choose. Although Peter's inability to make up his mind is portrayed as a sort of theoretical purgatory between ends and means, the important aspect of the novel is his final choice and why he makes it.

Peter's inner turmoil is the tale of vain efforts to find a moral compass in the modern world. His personal hell is due to the inability to link ends and means together into a rational model for political behavior. Literally washed ashore in a neutral country during the opening months of World War II, he is Koestler's prototype of modern man who has lost his intellectual, moral, and spiritual way in the contemporary world. Homeless, rootless, confused, with a discredited past and no future, Peter lives in a Hobbesian world where the avoidance of evil takes precedence over the pursuit of good.

There is a temptation to see the dilemma of Peter as the same that faced Rubashov. But Peter is in a very much different position than was Rubashov. Unlike the former, he has no Cartesian starting point from which to build a theoretical system. As a result of this difference, he confronts a greater array of theoretical temptations in the course of his pilgrimage through the novel. As with Rubashov, however, he is compelled by an inner need to think his thoughts out to their logical conclusions. Unlike Rubashov there is no predetermined path that his thoughts will follow to that end. The final outcome of his thought process, as well as its twists and turns along the way, remains somewhat in doubt until the very end.

The organization of *Arrival and Departure* is sufficiently different from Koestler's earlier work to merit comment. The organization is an integral part of the main points he is trying to make. In both *The Gladiators* and *Darkness at Noon*, Koestler was sensitive to the futurological structure of time in the commissar's world view. But he never systematically explored the place of time outside the commissar's conception. In *Arrival and Departure*, he makes the dimension of time one of the central features of his argument on the dilemmas of ends and means and relates it to the question of purpose in the human condition. The three chapters that form the heart of the work are entitled, in order of their sequence, "Present," "Past," and "Future." Framing these three are an opening and closing chapter entitled "Arrival" and "Departure." The importance of the sequence will become more apparant as the argument unfolds.

The style of *Arrival and Departure* is unmistakably that of Koestler—it is the struggle between and interplay of contending ideas. But this third novel adds a new dimension to this prior analysis of revolution—the possibility of a psychological motivation for political ideas that is wholly independent of those ideas themselves. Peter emerges from the novel as neither a yogi nor a commissar, but he is undoubtably an example of what Koestler sees as the political neurotic. But while he may be neurotic in Koestler's view, there is a truth in the vision that he argues that cannot be explained away by reductionist psychology or the commissar's police state.

I *The Arrival*

The geographical setting for the novel is the same as its political setting. The series of dialogues take place in the politically neutral country of Neutralia, a euphemism Koestler uses for Portugal, during the opening months of World War II. Peter arrives as a refugee from an unspecified East European country that has just been overrun by Fascists. He is literally washed ashore like a piece of driftwood. He can neither go back to his homeland nor easily escape from his present position. Neutralia is, like Peter, surrounded by a war over the future of Europe, yet takes no part in that war. This absence of political committment provides the perfect setting for Koestler's arguments. There is no significant physical action extraneous to his style. The arguments between competing ideologies thus take place at a purely theoretical level. Neutralia is a halfway house, midway between every ideological point on the political compass. The problem of political choice is therefore dependent on Koestler's perceptions of the theoretically rational aspects of choice.

Peter's status as an "ex"-member of the Communist party is more formal than is true beneath the surface. The party still retains a strong psychological and emotional hold on him. Upon his arrival he finds a tiny paper flag of the revolution on the beach and immediately fastens it to his lapel. It serves to give him the illusion of political identity in a country that shuns such identification. But the gesture is a hollow one. Both he and his former comrades, who have also taken temporary refuge in Neutralia, know that for all practical purposes he is outside the movement. He is linked to the party by his strong sense of idealism, but repelled and disillusioned by its practice. One anonymous comrade, her idealism still intact, remarks that "He was the hero of our generation." But she is instantly rebuked by her companion with the admonition: "what the revolution needs is not heroes but iron civil servants."[1] Outside the party, as Gletkin once reminded Rubashov, there is only oblivion.

Although Peter has no formal political affiliation, he is surrounded in Neutralia by every conceivable ideology. His lack of affiliation tends to make him an outcast among outcasts. To the Communists he is a hopeless romantic, looking for the ideal cause for which to become a martyr. To the other romantics, he is a hero of epic proportions—an idealist in a world of cynics. To still others he is a born loser, "itching to get himself into a new mess," forever destined "always to be on the losing side."[2] In addition to these preceptions by the outside world, the reader is also aware that Peter is something more than his outward characteristics—he is also haunted by an unspecified "evil dream" that lurks in the background of his political actions. He is a neurotic personality who is both politically and psychologically cripped by his past.

Peter's first act upon arrival in Neutralia is an unsucessful attempt to join the British Army. It is a time in the war when England is standing alone against the Nazis. Unfortunately for Peter, his past political affiliations make him undesirable to the British, and they turn down his request by a series of postponements. The British never actually say "no," and this has the effect of leaving him suspended in a kind of limbo that serves a symbolic function in the novel. Neutralia is as much a state of mind as geographic location. Events conspire to prevent his departure until he makes a political committment. Unattached to any political order in practice, Neutralia thus becomes a theoretical battleground among competing ideologies.

Politics are not ignored in Neutralia. On the contrary, there is little discussion of anything else. But such discussion is invariably abstract and theoretical. The practice of politics requires the departure of the theoreticians from Neutralia. But it also means that Neutralia is something akin to a state of nature, almost prepolitical. It is a place where Peter can begin his life anew. A substantial portion of Peter's intellectual odyssey, therefore, is an effort to see if there is any true alternative between Fascism and Communism. In the end he does finally join the British, but discovers even there that one cannot escape the dilemma of ends and means.

II *The Present*

The first step in Peter's efforts to think his thoughts to their logical conclusion is to establish a reference point in time from which to begin. Unlike Rubashov, he has cut himself off from the revolution and hence has no similar starting point. What is missing is a sense of purpose tied to a notion of the future. As a member of the party he had both a past and a future, but outside the party there is only an interminable present that is characterized by hopeless drift. Hence the reconstruction of a viable political theory begins of necessity with a reflection on the present. The dilemma of ends and means must first begin with an inquiry into the present condition of the European intellectual as Koestler sees him.

Pure reflection of this sort necessitates political inactivity in Koestler's view. Peter's position is therefore portrayed as a unique one among his experiences—he has never before been compelled to exist in an environment of pure ideas. The refugee environment symbolically drains Peter of all previous ideas so that he can start his intellectual life fresh. It is as if all prior conceptions must be erased before the new ones can be inscribed. The process of reconstructing a relationship between new theories and practices drains him both physically and emotionally.

At the time of his arrival in Neutralia, Peter is depicted as being debilitated by the twin effects of imprisonment by the Fascists and the intellectual trauma of being outside the party ranks. These two problems, one linked to his physical well-being and the other to his intellectual health, are inseparable in the novel. As he slowly regains his physical health, he also recovers his mental health; his relapse of the former is symptomatic of a dilemma of the psyche. The political point Koestler is making here is that the body politic cannot be expected to act rationally if its intellectual, that is, theoretical, faculties are disoriented. In the twentieth century, this means to Koestler that this relationship between thought and physical actions must be reconstituted on wholly new grounds. Peter's inability to link the two together is symptomatic of the greater crisis of Western thought. The outward inability of individuals to act rationally is the result of a theoretical confusion.

To assist in his theoretical recovery of health, modern man turns increasingly to science. It is the scientist who seems to stand above the value-laden political disputes of our time with an air of impartiality. The specific form of modern science that addresses itself to Peter's problem is psychology, in the figure of Dr. Sonia Bolgar. She is a refugee from the same country as Peter but with less of a passionate objection to Fascism. Her lack of political commitment is symbolic of science as a neutral arbitrator among competing values that it regards as of equal worth in the sense that all values are purely relative. Its choices from among these values are wholly arbitrary and cannot be rationally explained from within its own standards of measurement. Symbolically, Sonia is neither good nor bad. She represents both the best and the worst in modern science. Significantly, she is the first person in Neutralia to approach Peter with an offer of genuine help.

Dr. Bolgar and her rendition of psychology are the perfect represenatives of the eternal present. She is a hedonist of monumental proportions. She is absolutely convinced of the unreality of any other reference than the here and now. Reducing this reference point of the present to the point of philosophical absurdity, she tells Peter that there is more reality in a "mouthful of fruit than in the whole future."[3] And as befits a notion of time that only recognizes the reality of the present, Sonia is also without a past. She brags that she is like a rare tropical plant with roots in the air. Unlike Peter, she is as much at home in Neutralia as in her native land. Presumably, when she reaches America, her ultimate destination, she will be equally at home there.

What Peter finds most annoying about Sonia is her ability to remain politically neutral. Within the refugee community, she is a magnet to Communists and Fascists alike. She does not believe in anything beyond her own brand of psychology and believes it includes everything worth knowing about the nature of the human condition. Yet despite a certain measure of ideological unattractiveness, Peter and all the other refugees are irresistably drawn toward her. She is the only stable element in their lives. There is even an aura of mystery about her special science that fascinates even as it repells. "She was a specialist in that modern branch of confessional psychology and dream-surgery which made the secret obvious and surrounded the obvious with a halo of secrecy."[4] Her chief function in the modern world was to take over those duties and responsibilities previous centuries had reserved for priests.

The illusion of political neutrality was a source of comfort to many, and Dr. Bolgar helped to foster the notion that politics need not be taken too seriously. Her occasional visitors and patients included every stripe of political opinion. As a scientist she could make no distinctions between them. Her affect on Peter is to cause him to rethink all of his previous political ideas within the context of modern science as it applies to the study of the human condition. Her offer to help amounts to an effort to mold Peter into an image of herself. Her political neutrality meshes nicely with their mutual location in Neutralia, and as their stay is prolonged, Peter finds that this enforced neutrality causes the idea of past and future to lose their significance.[5]

For Peter, a life lived exclusively in and for the present is utterly at odds with his previous life. But in spite of its variance with life in the party, the world of the present is real nonetheless. The question is whether or not it is the only reality that matters politically. The longer Peter is under Sonia's spell, however, the less real other dimensions of time appear. As his understanding of purpose had been tied to the notion of a perfected future in the revolution, her attack on the idea of the future as a dimension of reality clearly undermines his revolutionary politics.

Peter's experience with the scientific present is intensified in his meething with Odette, one of Dr. Bolgar's patients, with whom he falls in love. Her presence in the novel is brief and serves mainly to provide a backdrop in making several other points. In certain respects, Odette personifies the dominance of the present over the future even more than does Sonia. Hers is an unreflective hedonism, whereas Sonia represents its philosophical justification. Koestler is aware that Sonia is the greater challenge, but he introduces Odette for two primary reasons: first, to show again the close link between thought and action, here represented symbolically by the relationship between intellectual and physical hedonism; and second, following Odette's sudden and unannounced departure for America, to provide a dramatic rupture between ideas and actions that is a hallmark of Koestler's world view. This latter purpose then enables Koestler to focus exclusively on theoretical problems for the remainder of the novel.

When Peter is cut off from sensuous gratification with the departure of Odette, he is forced to rethink all of his recently acquired notions of the present that Sonia has fed him. The first thing he discovers about himself is that he cannot ignore the past. As he begins the comparison of the past with the present, the latter is found wanting. The movement, even with all his doubts, seems in retrospect to have been more rational than either Sonia's present or his longing for Odette. That more rational past now compels him, seemingly against his will, to "make his passions crystalize into geometric patterns." Furthermore, his prior party indoctrination in abstract reasoning is the driving force behind his compulsion to think his thoughts through to their logical conclusion. It is a repetition of the same sort of compulsion of Rubashov but with the new twist that the end result does not consist in rejoining the party.

Peter's recollection of the party is one of "happy days, full of purpose and activity." It stands in sharp contrast with the empty present—empty, that is, of a purposeful future. In his past there was no disharmony between theory and practice. It stands apparently at the opposite end of the political spectrum as the present, and it leads him to ask the crucial question in the novel: Is it possible to act rationally in politics without a sense of theoretical purpose? Evidently the British, whom he wishes to join, can and are doing so in the skys over Britain. As he casually reads a popular account of an RAF pilot's story of the air war, Peter is struck by "the total lack of any inspired ideas behind [the English system]."[6] This lack of theoretical purpose behind the British war against Fascism is not only irrational, but is symptomatic of the overall moral and political decadance of the West in general. The only idea with spiritual vitality was Communism, but that had died in the law of detours.

Odette's departure for America thus serves as a catalyst for Peter's thoughts. Her abrupt exit serves to shock Peter into a conscious reevaluation of his entire life up to that point. Odette served, briefly, as Peter's firm anchor in the present, and he cannot escape its limitations until she leave, freeing him for pure thought. Considering her one-dimensional character, it is perhaps difficult to see just why her departure should have been so painful for Peter, since it is certainly less so to the reader. But her exit is the necessary first step in rebuilding an understanding of politics that can combine theory and practice.

On the very day of Odette's departure, Peter received word from the British consulate that his visa had finally arrived, permitting him to join the war against the Fascists. The two events are related; Odette's leaving forces Peter to consider acting politically, which in turn requires some calculation of past and future. On the surface it would appear that Peter finally has what he wanted all along. But this is deceptive. The departure of Odette forces him to make an immediate choice that is a characteristic dilemma for Koestler— whether to follow Odette to America and thus to choose political noncommittment in an eternal present, or to go to England and dedicate himself to a political activism that is without theoretical underpinnings. The dilemma is a tacit admission that alternative futures do exist, that they are not totally determined, and that they are dependent on his own actions. But before he can decide upon a future, he must first come to terms with his own past.

III   *The Past*

The choice between alternate futures begins with an understanding of the past. Here Peter is presented with a classical Koestlerian dilemma, a choice between two entirely separate paths that are both theoretical blind alleys and yet superficially attractive. To follow Odette and remain politically neutral, or to join the British and foresake political rationality. Though the dilemma is intended to portray a real problem and not merely an abstract one, it nevertheless

appears contrived in a practical sense. Its value is that it enables
Koestler to explore the theoretical arguments unobstructed by physical action.

Much like Spartacus, Peter first reacts with indecision. But unlike
Spartacus, that indecision overwhelms him completely. He cannot
resolve the matter by default because he is suspended in Neutralia,
between the yogi and the commissar. To make no decision is to stay in
Neutralia. Spartacus' indecision was political because of its context,
while Peter's is apolitical for the same reason. It is neutrality that
permits a paralysis of will that would not otherwise be possible. "The
mere idea of moving, of performing practical actions, filled him with
. . . panic."[7]

This paralysis of political will is paralleled by a physical paralysis of
Peter's right leg. The physical malfunction has its origins in his
psychological disorders. The significance of the dilemma goes beyond the relationship of thought to action. It appears as a problem
that only Sonia is capable of solving. Only science seems to offer a
solution.

The task of Sonia in the recovery of Peter's mental health is to
reconstruct his past and exorcise it of its demons. It is nothing less
than a reconstruction of Peter's history stripped of all illusions and
pretenses. It is then to be reassembled as a wholly rational unfolding
of cause and effect in the idiom of scientific determinism. At the end
of her analysis, she concludes that given his environmental stimulus,
Peter could not have acted any differently than he in fact did. It is a
tautological explanation, but one that Koestler regards as endemic in
the deterministic side of science. Its greatest weakness is that scientific determinism does not coincide with Peter's experience with
free-willed choice that has led him to his present impass in the first
place. There is an obvious lag between science as it understands itself
theoretically and as it is experienced by outsiders. It is a theme
Koestler returns to almost thirty years later in *The Call–Girls*.

Lacking any commitment to transcendent values herself, Sonia is
completely unable to understand their presence in Peter except as
the consequence of a disturbed psyche.

Courage. . . . Devotion. . . . Self-sacrifice. . . . I don't use any of those
words. They belong to the dramatic vocabulary of prophets—though I am
told even they occasionally had foam at the mouth. I merely wanted to say
that in this age all crusaders are stigmatised. They try to hide it by being
doctrinaire, or matter of fact and tough, but when they are alone and naked
they all sweat little drops of blood through their skin.[8]

Peter is no different in her estimation. She knows that deep in the recesses of his psyche there is the "evil dream" that is somehow at the bottom of his idealism. It has made him an enigma both to himself and to others. At different times and under different circumstances, it has made him a coward one moment and a hero the next. All of his talk about ideals and noble purposes in revolutionary activism are a cover for a neurotic guilt complex.

Under Sonia's relentless probing, it turns out that Peter's evil dream stems from guilt feelings toward a younger brother. It is a classic Freudian example of the transference of a problem in one area to the symbolization of it in another—in this case from a personal sin onto politics. Originally Peter had been jealous of the younger brother, and then after an accident in which the latter lost an eye, that same jealousy turned to guilt over the original jealousy. He felt a sense of sin for which he should have been punished but was not. Later, when tortured by the Fascists, he took it as an atonement for the earlier sin. That guilt was only increased when the movement mistook his act of masochism for bravery. What the party regarded as heroism was in reality only an acute neurosis.

What science demonstrates to Peter is that both heroism and cowardice stem from the same source—the sick mind. Thus do the ultimately moral decisions in politics dissolve into a morass of neurotic personalities transfering their own peculiarities onto the political world. The problem that Koestler now confronts as a result of Sonia's science is an exceedingly difficult one—how to point out the short comings of psychology as *the* science of the human condition and at the same time to retain the core of its truth. Sonia, after all, is not entirely wrong in her diagnosis. There is an unquestionably neurotic element in Peter. Furthermore, by bringing it out into the open she lays the groundwork for its cure. "Under Sonia's guidance Peter began to find his way in this weird and yet familiar world; her patient dream-surgery laid bare the roots of his shame and pride, of his self-accusations and craving for explanation. . . . He had grown very fond of her, and dependent on her."[9] It is important, however, that while Sonia can bring Peter to the brink of recovery, she cannot consumate it. That final phase is entirely up to Peter. The physical paralysis, the inability to act politically, is found to be an act of personal will. But ultimately Sonia's inability to work a cure is very much bound up with her success in diagnosing the trouble. In the systematic and total destruction of Peter's value system, she has also severed the unity of theory and practice necessary to a complete recovery. How can he act, Koestler asks, if there is no rational reason to act in any particular way? Before he can completely recover physically, there must be something to fill the void left by modern science in his value structure.

The destruction of all sense of purpose by modern science is vividly portrayed in Peter's reaction to his supposed cure. His past may have been built on illusions, but at least they were the basis for actions. Now, however, his "once firm beliefs in values became fluid and dissolved into their chemical components."[10] Everything had been explained away as a form of neurosis. He now finds himself in a state of intellectual infancy in which progress toward maturity requires a complete reconstruction of a philosophy and science of politics. Furthermore, this reconstruction will have to take cognizance of the discoveries of modern science however destructive it may seem. The same science that destroys the past also promises a new tomorrow even as it denies the notion that there will be a tomorrow. But the immediate effect of science is to destroy the past and to leave nothing in its place. The danger of that "nothing" is that it threatens to become a pure nihilism.

There is no doubt but that the destruction of Peter's past is absolute; "under Sonia's influence the proud structure of values had collapsed." At this point, Peter's necessity to continue alone calls into question the validity or the value of the cure. His leg is still paralyzed, and he wonders if in fact the evil dream has been purged from his psyche. If science had really effected a cure, "why did not everything become clear and simple now; why was his leg still smitten by the edge of the sword."[11] The loss of the past is at first unbearable, and Peter initially turned against Sonia, but it is only temporary. He still needs her to help him travel the last step.

The last stumbling block in his scientific cure is the discovery by Sonia that he could never say to his father, "Forgive me." It is an essentially religious symbolism. His father, like the God of the desert, is long since dead. Still, he must make a symbolic act of penance and confess his sins before he can be released from the bondage of the past. This done, Peter experiences a "rapture of sudden understanding" that causes, mystically, the last piece of this giant jigsaw puzzle to fall into place. At last he can move his leg. As yet he has not come to terms with any particular future, but with his past now rationalized it becomes the next logical step.

Within the symbolic context of Peter's cure, Koestler is making several political points. First, even though politics is future-oriented, the past still plays a role, although it is essentially a negative one. The hold of that past built on illusions must be broken before the future can truly begin. Second, while this process can be assisted by science, in the final analysis, modern science cannot link together thought with action because modern science is essentially destructive. Yet science is all there is left of rationality in the modern world, and somehow it must be made to work.

The effect of Sonia's cure on Peter is at first like a tonic. His entire world view changes. "At last the future lay open to him. He had shaken off the fetters of the past—fictitious allegiances, imaginary debts." The route toward a new future was unencumbered by any past whatever; "he could do whatever he liked."[12] But while this marked the end of politics as a crusade in the manner of a commissar, it was not the end of politics. He still faced the problem of building a future as an act of individual will. The best he could say of the past was that thanks to modern science it was no longer an obstacle to progress and had simply become irrelevant.

IV *The Future*

In the aftermath of Peter's scientific cure, the dilemmas of political choice reassert themselves in the same form as before he had erased his past. Science has affected a physical cure, but it is a superficial one. Peter cannot be pronounced completely cured until he returns to political life. He must still decide whether to follow Odette to America or to join the British. Since Sonia also leaves for America at this time, his final choice will have to be made in isolation. It is when he is by himself that the superficial nature of the scientific cure becomes most evident. Science cannot answer the question of "why" in politics, and in this final chapter the dilemma of choice turns on the problem of purpose.

Peter's first doubts come when he reconsiders the methodology of Sonia's science: "Was there a flaw in Sonia's method, in spite of its ingenious subtlety? The malignant growth had been cut out but the operation seemed to have left deeper scars than could be accounted for. She had promised to restore his appetite for life, but instead he experienced only pangs of greed, alternating with weary satiety."[13]

Although Peter is presented as having decided initially to follow Odette to America, this must be seen as serving a literary function— that of allowing Koestler to explore a variety of alternative futures that now present themselves to Peter. The contrast with Rubashov here is striking. Rubashov could never find his way out of the commissar's labyrinth because of the determinism of the party ideology. Peter, on the other hand, has been freed from determinism by a science that has heavy overtones of determinism. It is one of the ironies of modern science that it undermines determinism even while adopting a deterministic methodology. Peter's future is freer than either Spartacus' or Rubashov's in large part because of the very science that must now be questioned.

What emerges from the closing pages of *Arrival and Departure* is the notion that the dilemma of choice itself may be the greatest political reality men face, perhaps even equal to the choices themselves. Peter's freedom to chose alternative futures comes down to a choice among four that are mutually contradictory: to rejoin the party, to follow Odette to America, to join the Facists, or to join the British. The first is rejected because it would mean the dominance of the past over his life again. The second is apolitical, and the reader never really expects him to follow it. As for joining the Fascists, Peter experiences the arguments in the person of Bernard, a local Fascist, but never the temptation to join, in spite of the fact that the social experiments in Nazi Germany are quite similar to the mass upheavals in Communist society. Since that leaves only the option of joining the British as a viable alternative, the question is not whether he will join them or not, but "why."

Since his decision to join the British is the act of will that consumates his spiritual recovery, Koestler's interpretation of it is crucial to understanding the message of the novel. Since the novel is set in 1940—the same year, incidentally, that Koestler left Portugal for England—it cannot be said that any decision will be based on any certainty that England will prevail. Here England represents a halfway house in the West, caught between the extremes of Fascism and Communism. It offers no inspiring utopia of the future for which to fight that still excites Peter's imagination. The choice is made, therefore, in full recognition of the fatal rupture of theory and practice in the modern world. Given the fact of this split, the choice is on the side of practice rather than theoretical consistancy. This too is a change from Spartacus and Rubashov.

The British representatives in Neutralia offer sharply contrasting forecasts of the future that may await Peter by chosing the path he does. One is a Mr. Wilson, the British consulate. He is middle-aged, flabby, and with a touch of the gout. The other is Andrew, a former RAF pilot who is the military attache with the consulate. Andrew has been horribly mutilated in the air war and is now grounded because of his wounds. He is a physical monster because of the war, but he still retains an intellectual dimension and he fascinates Peter as does no other person in Neutralia. He is a symbol of the casual English heroism without a purpose that had registered itself so forcefully on Peter earlier. Between the gout-ridden Mr. Wilson and the deformed Andrew, the British would not seem to be particularly attractive futures. Yet between them they shatter his decision to follow Odette.

It is Andrew who most convinces Peter of the flaws in Sonia's science. She had argued in effect that because a thing could be explained it could also be justified in a deterministic sense. But this was the fatal weakness of the argument: "She would not have approved of his accepting Bernard's offer. But from what source did she derive her disapproval? Where was there room in her system for such discrimination? She was a great uprooter of trees; had she not torn out of her garden the tree of knowledge of good and evil? Was not her aim to go back to the time before the fall?"[14]

Peter's discovery of what he preceives to be the weakness of Sonia's argument brings him full circle, to the time in the past when he first joined the party. Knowledge means the discrimination between good and evil. The choice between the two is what politics is all about. But as Bernard had reminded him, in the modern world there are no neat lines of trenches in the warfare of ideas, and the distinction between friend and foe is hopelessly blurred. The choice of England even as a temporary future is one of pure action over theory and is spiced with a strong dose of pessimism as a result. It means to Peter that he has accepted the irrationality of political actions in the modern world. It is Andrew who sums up this attitude best when he says to Peter, "Don't you think it is a rather boring game, trying to find one's reasons for doing something."[15] The importance of Andrew's insight on Peter's decision could scarcely be overestimated: "And that was the difference between his first crusade which had ended with his breakdown on Sonia's couch, and the second on which he now departed. The first time he had set out in ignorance of his reasons; this time he knew them, but understood that reasons do not matter so much."[16]

Peter then explains his choice in terms of a quasi-religious notion of purpose that is divorced from reason but which is the other side of Koestler's own rationalism. In what Peter saw as the "dynamics of history," the British stood for values that had gone musty and for the power of the status quo and the past. They were no longer the engine of progress they had once been, but rather its brakes; "But when the engine became overheated and began to run wild, there was need for a brake."[17] While the British cannot act morally in politics from Peter's view, they can at least avoid acting immorally. But to make this halfway house philosophy palatable, it is endowed with a mysticism reminiscent of religious experience, the same sort of oceanic feeling described by Rubashov.

Mysticism is described by Peter in the form of a short story he writes, which is included in the final pages of *Arrival and Departure*. It is a separate story within the novel, but one that illuminates an important aspect of Koestler's work. The story is entitled "The Last Judgement" and is an allegorical tale of God's judgement on sins of omission and comission in politics. Symbolically, it is judgement on the yogi and the commissar along with the halfway houses in between. The story is perhaps the dramatic highpoint of the novel.

"The Last Judgement" is an example of Koestler's writing at its best. Although he does it only rarely in his works, Koestler is a master at this sort of allegorical writing. As the story relates to Peter's decision, two points are made. The first is that every day lived in the eternal present is a day of "last judgement." Past, present, and future are thus melded into a single dimension of time, and the distinction loses its analytic validity. Purpose, therefore, is understood as bringing together these three components of time in the human condition. Second, everyone is guilty of something—the yogi for sins of omission and the commissar for sins of comission. Yet the punishment for those sins seems to bear no relation to the magnitude of the sins themselves. Furthermore, what punishment there is comes not from God, who is conspicuously absent from the last judgement, but from other men who appear to have taken His place. In the trial scene that Koestler conjures up, there is a surrealistic scene of the accused and accusors that is reminiscent of the trial in Kafka. It is a judicial process marked not by a rule of law, but by a process that is the very essence of arbitrary yet just decisions. But in spite of the severe or light sentences handed down, none of them is ever carried out. Each day the accused return to the trial, where the charade of the preceeding day is reenacted. It is an endless and perpetual cycle that extends indefinitely into an unknown future.

What the story points toward for Koestler is the breakdown of the binding effect of both morality and law in the modern world. Without God to pronounce the last judgement, the entire process is a nightmarish experience in chaos. The death of God has caused the collapse of any ordering principles by which a knowledge of good and evil may be made. Political choice thereby is irrational of its very nature. With the breakdown of reason, Peter can only make his choice on the basis of a mysticism that seems at first to be utterly at odds with Koestler's earlier writing, yet upon closer inspection is wholly consistant with them.

V *Departure*

Peter's departure from Neutralia has struck many critics as anticlimactic. It has seemed to be unrelated to the rest of the novel and to be merely a postscript designed to get him out into the war. A closer reading of *Arrival and Departure*, however, suggest a different explanation. It is related to the mystical irrationality that lies beneath the surface of the heavy rationalism that has attracted the attention of most critics. It is a theme more obvious in *The Gladiators'* vision of the "death of God" than in *Darkness at Noon* where the theme was less conspicuous.

Given the absence of absolute standards for the judgement of political morality, what does one do? Peter's answer is to plunge back into the political chaos on the side of the uninspiring British. It is an act that seems to be in response to Ivanov's assertion in *Darkness at Noon* that it is Satan who brings order out of a chaotic universe. Peter, suspended halfway between heaven and hell, tries to bring an order out of that same chaos that is neither demonic, as in the case of the commissar, nor saintly, as in the case of the yogi. It is a Promethian act that has much in common with the idea of the rebel in Camus. Peter's return to the chaos of war amounts to Koestler's version of a perfect self-sacrafice, in a Christlike gesture, that may offer some hope for the future. In his closing letter to Odette, explaining the reasons for his choice as best he can, Peter offers his vision of a hope that seems oddly out of place in terms of Koestler's *Darkness at Noon*. But it is a consistant theme in most of his other writing: "I'll tell you my belief, Odette, I think a new god is about to be born. That is the kind of thing one is allowed to say only at certain moments; but this is the moment. . . . Praise to the unborn god. . . . Don't try to divine his message or the form of his cult—this will be after our time. . . . For we are all the last descendents of Renaissance-man, the end and not the beginning."[18]

In this sort of statement, the reader can hear an echo of the Essene, Spartacus, and even of Rubashov in his own way. There is a premonition of the role science was to play in Koestler's later work. But the apparent optimism of a new god about to be born does not ring quite true. Peter is portrayed at the end as a hero, but he is a hero at a time when modern politics have destroyed the very notion of a hero. Without a god, as he recognizes, with which he can measure his accomplishments and failures, he cannot know for certain whether he is a hero or merely a fool. In this doubt, combined with decisive political action, Peter is Koestler's version of the paradigmatic tough-minded intellectual for the emerging world. He is idealistic in the face of cynicism, pessimistic in the face of optimism. Neither yogi nor commissar, he is a man stripped of adolescent fantasies about good and evil, yet retaining a quality of childlike innocence. He is a bundle of loose ends and contradictons who has learned to act politically and to chose between expediency and morality.

CHAPTER 6

In the Shadow of the Neanderthals

*T*he *Age of Longing*, which appeared in 1951, was the last of Koestler's major fiction writing for two decades. It was apparently intended to be his last argument on politics in the mold of the yogi and the commissar. Most of Koestler's critics have considered it to have been one of his most flawed pieces, second only to *Thieves in the Night*. While it is not without some stylistic and organizational problems, *The Age of Longing* is a better novel than most critics have been willing to recognize. In addition, *The Age of Longing* is an important transitional work between Koestler's career as a novelist and his later scientific writing. Both phases are basically of a piece, and it is this novel that helps to tie them together.

The basic theme of *The Age of Longing* is the political and spiritual collapse of Europe in the aftermath of World War II. The story is set in Paris sometime in the late 1950s where the characters live in imminent expectation of a third world war sparked by the Soviet Union. The novel was composed during the zenith of Stalin's postwar power and captures the pessimism of the anti-Communist Left perhaps better than any other work of the period. It is probably the most pessimistic of all Koestler's writing, unrelieved by even a glimmer of philosophical optimism at the end.

In its fundamental outlines, the political dilemma of *The Age of Longing* is classic Koestler vintage; it is political argument on a purely theoretical level in which the different actors are unable to act rationally because of theoretical confusion. Because the main characters are unable to chose rationally from among competing alternatives, political indecision is the result, and by default, the lack of action tends to favor the Soviet Union. The political dilemma of *The Age of Longing* is the closest Koestler ever comes in his writing to depicting a genuine tragedy. It is tragic in the classical sense because the final, inevitable outbreak of war between Russia and the West seems as predictable as it is avoidable. What is lacking in the West is the will to resist totalitarianism. The spiritual strength of the West has been dissipated not only by the effects of World War II, but also by the ascendency of a secular spirit that has drained it of the capacity to make moral decisions. The figures in the novel, regardless of their political ideas, live with a sense of longing for a vanished past made all the more attractive by the present dread of a seemingly inevitable barbaric future.

The political dialogues are haunted by a gloomy pall cast over Paris from Stalinist Russia. The Communist ideology of revolution now has a hollow and somewhat tired ring that is in sharp contrast with the vitality of the same arguments in *Darkness at Noon*. A few of the intellectuals are sensitive to the threat and know that barbarism is just around the corner in the form of the heirs of Gletkin but are utterly unable to do anything about it. The party represents a modern version of Neanderthals, but Paris intellectual life has become so decadant that to many the party types look like an advanced species.

The novel opens on Bastille Day in Paris, the birthday of democratic government in France. But there is a dread that animates the city, as many fear that freedom is about to be extinguished. A Monsieur Anatole, at whose home the day is being celebrated, sets the mood early in the novel: "Who knows . . . it may be our last Bastille Day before the advent of the Neanderthal. Or the last-but-one, the last-but-two; what is the difference? The people of Pompeii were lucky: they did not know beforehand."[1]

As the dialogues develop, the reasons for the barbarism of modern politics becomes increasingly apparant. It is a direct consequence of the secularization of society, following in the wake of the "death of God" syndrome. Society has become the new god, but it is a god that still leaves a spiritual void in men's hearts. All that can be done now is to lament the passing of the old god, the dessert God of the Essene in *The Gladiators*, and to mourn his passing. It is never certain in *The Age of Longing* whether this past was ever more than an illusion, but it is certain that certain illusions are preferable to real barbarisms. Here the overall pessimism of Koestler in this work is in contrast to his occasional optimism in his earlier novels. The future in *The Age of Longing* most certainly belongs to the new barbarians and not to the new god that Peter envisioned or the Christ around the corner from the gladiators. But the most catastrophic aspect of this barbarism is that it is immanent.

The specific time frame in *The Age of Longing* is most important for an interpretation of the novel. The story is set in the late 1950s. Since the novel appeared in 1951, this means that the story is set only slightly in the future. The events are familiar enough to give the impression of reading tomorrow's newspaper headlines. In contrast to *Nineteen Eighty-Four*, for example, the setting has an immediate sense of urgency and not the surrealistic quality that comes from casting the story far into the future. The structure of time in the novel gives it a prophetically apocalyptic tone that is lacking in his other novels.

Parisian intellectual life in the novel is intended to be a microcosm of modern Europe. There is an aura of genteel decadence that stands in sharp contrast with the vitality of "The Commonwealth of Freedomloving People," Koestler's euphemism for the Soviet Union. This deliberately misleading name gives it a slightly Orwellian touch of newspeak. This "Free Commonwealth," as it is popularly called, determines the shape of political arguments, not the West. Actions are perceived as rational or irrational solely on the grounds of whether or not they might antagonize the Free Commonwealth. But all such arguments prove in the end to have been purely academic, as war comes in spite of Western appeasement.

It is an integral part of Koestler's message that the final political decisions that affect Europe's survival are made in Washington and Moscow but not in Paris. The Europeans have lost control of their own destiny. All that is left for them is to argue politics abstractly in the cafes and salons of their cities since they cannot act politically. It is significant to note that the only two characters who are able to act are Hydie, an American, and Feyda, a Russian spy.

The intellectual arguments are held together by the general notion, as one character puts it, that Europe is "going to the dogs." Although there is ample diversity of opinion as to why this is so, the final reason seems to be the spiritual decadence wrought by secularization.

Because this secularization of politics is closely tied to the notion of science in Koestler's writing, *The Age of Longing* may be viewed as a bridge to his later work on science. The problem of science arises for Koestler when he begins to look into the structure of reason and knowledge that lies behind the dilemma of political choice. This is a far larger problem than that of the yogi and the commissar alone. In *The Age of Longing*, there is a far greater sense of uncertainty as to where reason resides in the modern world. Feyda, the commissar figure in the novel, does not argue revolution with the same vitality as

Spartacus, Rubashov, or even Peter. Implicity in the novel there is
the recognition that before political theories can be joined to rational
action, the entire understanding of scientific knowledge must be
thought through to its logical conclusions. It means that the yogi-
commissar continuum is insufficient by itself to contain the whole of
the political dilemma. When this aspect of the novel is compared with
Koestler's subsequent writing, it is perhaps easier to see why fiction
was no longer the best medium in which to explore the problem.

The political dialogues in *The Age of Longing* are a series of abstract
and yet important arguments between a wide variety of political
types. Indeed, there is more diversity of political opinion here than
anywhere else in Koestler's novels. That is both the strength and the
weakness of the novel. There is no single figure or analytic framework
as tight as the yogi-commissar concept to hold the dialogues together.
Three individuals, however, do stand out more than any of the
others, and the most important points in the novel are expressed
through them or in response to them. The bulk of the narrative
revolves around their lives. The three are, Hydie Anderson, a
generally witless American who is probably one of the least satisfactory characters in Koestler's fiction; Feyda Nikitin, a secret police
agent for the Free Commonwealth who early becomes Hydie's lover;
and Julien Delattre, another of Koestler's disillusioned ex-party
members, a former French Resistance fighter during World War II
and perhaps the closest Koestler ever came to creating his own alter
ego in literary form. The numerous minor figures seldom take on a life
of their own, with a few exceptions, and generally serve as foils for the
three principle characters. Each of the main characters represents a
wholly different background of experiences in the modern world, and
yet all are tied together by the bond of a common political
dilemma—a political milieu that is inherently irrational. Their inter-
relationships with one another and the lesser characters form the core
of the political drama as it theoretically develops.

I   *Hydie*

Unlike most of Koestler's other literary creations, the figure of
Hydie embodies experience more than ideas. It is not so much what
she says that is important, but rather her actions and experience.
Whereas the reader is drawn to Koestler's other literary creations by
the sheer force of their ideas, in Hydie that same attention is directed
toward her unique yet vaguely commonplace experiences. She has
few political ideas, and those she does have are more emotional than

rational. When her political conscience is finally awakened at the end of the novel, it remains an emotional rather than rational conscience.

Although some have considered Hydie to exemplify Koestler's literary prowess at is nadir, she is perhaps one of his most interesting and yet improbable characters. First of all, she is one of the few Americans to appear anywhere in his fiction. Second, as Koestler concentrates on her actions over her experience, an added dimension is opened up in his commentary on the relationship of theory to practice. It could be said that she is a parody of Americans in general and that, hence, her political naivete is Koestler's drole commentary on America. But in his miscellaneous essays of the same period there is no such hint of a parody of America. A more likely interpretation would suggest that she is less naive than innocent in politics. Her loss of genuine innocence comes with the combination of Parisian intellectual life and her encounter with Feyda. American political innocence lost is evidently believable in the early 1950s, whereas an innocent European must strike Koestler as wholly improbable.

The experiences that order Hydie's thoughts and actions are twofold. First is her experience of a religious conversion to Catholicism, followed by her apostasy during World War II. In this she represents the cycle of Western civilization as it is viewed from the twentieth century. Second is her decision to take Feyda as her lover, which in turn determines much of the flow of the story. The love affair is set against a backdrop of international tension and intrigue, the substance of which she remains blissfully unaware of until the very end.

On the surface, Hydie resembles most of Koestler's fictional characters. She is disillusioned with politics and adrift without rational or moral convictions. In her religious apostasy, she has lost faith in moral absolutes of the past and can find nothing to replace them. She is drifting in an eternal present without hope of a purposeful future. But beneath this surface appearance, Hydie is strikingly different from the other "ex"-believers in Koestler's novels. Her disillusionment with politics stems directly from a religious and not a political apostasy. Her original experience with conversion to a creed was religious and not political. In terms of the yogi and the commissar, her original point on the analytic continuum was that of the yogi. Her present disillusionment is halfway between the yogi and the commissar, as was Peter's in *Arrival and Departure*, but she began her pilgrimage from the opposite end of the spectrum. The point is that despite her different origins, she now stands on the same spot.

In her conversion to a religious creed as well as her later apostasy, Koestler intends to provide a contrast with both his earlier work in general and Feyda in particualr. Although the substance of religious and political creeds may vary, the conversion experience itself emerges as the same phenomonon to the individual involved. Feyda stands out in this comparison in that while she loses her faith, he does not. In the modern world, faith in the revolution is stronger than faith in God. Belief in something, no matter what it may be, is stronger than faith in nothing. What Hydie has in common with the others, except Feÿda, is a longing for a now dead faith that was once a part of their common past. Without such faith, Hydie winds her way through most of the novel as a "political chamelion." Having no fixed values of her own, she tends to take on the political coloration of whoever is around her; she has "No core, no faith, no fixed values."[2]

To understand the basic experience that now orders Hydie's life is to begin with her conversion and subsequent apostasy. In Koestler's version, that experience is more rational than mystical, in spite of his best efforts to recreate a sort of "oceanic experience" around it. She was, Koestler tells us, in her youth "obsessed with the problem of sainthood."[3] But that obsession takes the form of an intellectual wrestling with an abstract problem. This is partly due to Koestler's skepticism of the reality of saints. But primarily it is because he sees the problem of morality in rational terms more than mystical terms. Sainthood may not be real for Koestler, but Hydie's struggle with morality is real. The plane upon which she struggles is, in Koestler's view, a political one, and it is her failure to understand its dimension that is at the root of her difficulty. Concern with religious sainthood is of its very nature apolitical; it has the effect of removing the person from the political world of real choices. Hydie's concern with individual perfection as opposed to social perfection leads her to a convent where she is in effect guilty of sins of omission in the world outside.

Ultimately, Hydie's purely intellectualized religion proves to be the source of its collapse. Reason does not support religion in the modern world. Had her conversion been truly mystical, it might have survived the rationalist assault. Religious faith, as Koestler describes it, depends upon the a priori acceptance of a rational and purposeful universe. Such assumptions, he believes, may be beyond the ability of science to prove or disprove, but given the history of the twentieth century, it has become a doubtful proposition. It is World War II that will destroy Hydie's faith: "as nothing could happen without His will, and as those things kept happening, the only explanation was that

God suffered from some malignant form of insanity."[4] It is significant to point out here that it is her contact with the political world outside the convent that causes the crisis of her religious faith: "The dreadful thing is not the suffering itself, but the pointlessness of it."[5]

Hydie's conversion to Catholicism came from an obsession with sainthood. That antipolitical obsession, however, could not withstand the contradictions between personal and social morality. Her dilemma is basically that of the yogi. In the political world she discovered the maxim of Saint-Just, quoted by Koestler in the frontpiece to *Darkness at Noon:* "Nobody can rule guiltlessly." Political noninvolvement, in other words, cannot rationally survive contact with the social mileu. A religious life, as Koestler understands the term, is not possible in the modern world.

To dramatize the difference between Hydie's faith in a religious creed and Feyda's faith in a political one, Koestler places the chapters dealing with their respective faith conversions back to back. The contrast is striking. Because Feyda never loses faith in the political utopia of the future, he never experiences the rupture between theory and practice that is the bane of Hydie's experience in religion. His faith is as much a source of strength as her faith is a source of weakness. Her prayer, "LET ME BELIEVE IN SOMETHING," is unanswered, whereas Feyda's secularized purpose is fulfilled. There are no saints in Koestler's political world.

For most of the novel Hydie is Feyda's lover. This is during her apolitical phase, when she is disillusioned with the political world. Curiously, her break with Feyda comes not over a specifically political issue but over the implications of his applied behavioral psychology. In this there is an echo of Peter's reaction to Sonia in *Arrival and Departure.* For most of the novel, Hydie and Feyda debate what seem to her abstract points of political theory. Though she argues against him, she always has the nagging feeling that he may be right. After all, he is certain of his beliefs, while she is not. It is an attitude similar to Rubashov's ambivalence toward No. 1.

It is Hydie's realization that she had been a mere object in their love affair that leads to her split with Feyda. His crude application of behavioral stimulus-response on her comes as a revelation: "she knew she had been humilated past anything a drunken customer might inflict on a prostitute."[6] She does not reason out the "why" of the humiliation—it is something beyond pure reason. It is her personal discovery of her own "grammatical fiction."

Feyda, for his part, is utterly unable to comprehend her sense of humiliation. Humiliation implies a degree of personhood beyond anything that can be ordered into his materialistic universe. Koestler's point is a repetition of earlier themes—that for all the weight of evidence and reason that modern science has marshalled to support materialism, fundamental human experience rebels against it. But it is only the commissar's particular version of science that is at issue. Properly understood, science in the twentieth century has undermined that Newtonian world view and at least points to a way past some of the commissar dilemmas. Koestler's subsequent scientific writing should be seen as his detailed rebuttal to the commissar and at least a partial way around the impass of the yogi and the commissar. What he questions is not science *per se,* but rather what he sees as a mistaken view of it.

Hydie's emotional response to Feyda is interesting for several reasons. In his previous work, Koestler had implicitly, and sometimes explicitly, argued that the challenge of the commissar could only be met on the theoretical level. Yet Hydie's response is both morally correct and meets with Koestler's approval. This emotional response would seem to be outside of the yogi-commissar continuum that had previously dominated the structure of rationality in Koestler's novels. The explanation for this departure from previous patterns would appear to be twofold. One is that in the early 1950s Koestler perceived the Soviet military threat against Western Europe to be so grave that immediate action was called for, irrespective of theoretical considerations. The other is more subtle and far reaching in terms of Koestler's development as a writer—the yogi-commissar continuum could no longer contain the whole of political reality in his world view, although it continued to be the major single influence. His study of modern science later can also be seen as a modfication, though not an abandonment, of that earlier framework.

Hydie's emotional response to Feyda at the time of their break is politically irrational despite its morality. For reasons that are not entirely explained, her humiliation from the application of behaviorism causes the scales to fall from her eyes regarding Feyda's spy mission in Paris. She now understands what everyone else already knew, that this job for the Free Commonwealth is to prepare a list of persons to be liquidated following the Communist takeover. Initially she turns to her father, an American army officer attached to the embassy in a counterespionage assignment. When he cannot take any action against Feyda, she turns to Julien and finally to the police. Her assumption is that if everyone knew what Feyda was doing, he would be immediately arrested. But as it turns out, they already knew or at least suspected Feyda's mission. They all respond with a polite boredom and wonder why it has taken her so long to discover the obvious. At that point Hydie decides that the only rational course of action is to take matters into her own hands and kill Feyda.

The inability of society around her to respond to the genuine threat from the Free Commonwealth is the direct result of the spiritual collapse of Europe. Sophistic arguments, barely believed by their own advocates, have undermined the physical and moral ability of Europe to defend itself. It raises the question of just how irrational Hydie's action is. There is at least the possibility that her response is the most rational of all, that what is rational or irrational may only appear that way because of the environment in which actions take place. Is it more rational to stand idly by and do nothing while a new wave of barbarians sweep over what used to be considered the most cultured city in Europe?

Whether rational or irrational, Hydie's attempted assassination of Feyda is both futile and abortive. She hasn't the slightest idea of how to use the pistol she has procured to do the job. In order to insure that her actions are not interpreted as those of a woman scorned, she determines not to try and hide her culpability for the deed. She anticipates that her action will awaken the West from its political stupor by the resulting publicity. Unfortunately, for Hydie at least, she thoroughly bungles the attempt at murder and manages merely to wound Feyda. The affair turns into more of an embarassment for all the parties concerned than a political act. The entire episode is kept officially quiet.

What Koestler is trying to portray here is a symbolic act of political expediency in the name of morality, an act in which the end will justify the means. Yet it is not the action of a commissar. That it proves abortive is symptomatic of the difficulty the West faces in dealing with the Soviet menace. While many critics have seen this episode as a distraction that borders on the frivolous, it is an important part of the novel's symbolism. Koestler does not manage the symbolism as effectively as in other novels, but it is not thereby irrelevant to his purposes. The weakness of the symbolism is probably due more to its being linked to a female character than to the act itself. Feminine portraits are not Koestler's best literary creations, and Hydie is no exception. The futile gesture can easily be misinterpreted as a fiasco by a mindless American schoolgirl. The bungled attempt ultimately weakens the impact on the reader of Feyda's mission.

Inadvertently, Koestler seems to engender a measure of sympathy for Feyda, who is not a sympathetic figure, and of contempt for Hydie, who is not a contemptible person. Much of the importance of the most dramatic point of the novel in terms of its action is lost when Koestler fails to tie the act specifically into a large framework.

II *Feyda*

Despite the centrality of Hydie to the novel as a whole, by far the most interesting figure is Feyda Nikitin. The main reason seems to be that Koestler is at the height of his literary prowess in describing what he has called the commissar mentality. In these portraits Koestler has few peers among contemporary writers.

Feyda is undoubtably Koestler's most finely drawn commissar after Rubashov in *Darkness at Noon*. His closest counterpart in personality, however, is Gletkin. Indeed, Feyda is introduced as a protege of Gletkin. It was Koestler's intention that he represent a more mature version of Gletkin. Feyda is a deeper personality than Gletkin and, unlike Koestler's earlier character, he is something more than what he seems to be on the surface. In *Darkness at Noon*, the reader had only a few glimpses into Gletkin's past, and it was left to his imagination to reconstruct what that past might have been. In *The Age of Longing*, Feyda's past is explored as deeply as Hydie's or as that of Rubashov earlier. Feyda is as much a "repellant creature" as was Gletkin, but here this is as much a product of his complexity as the masters he serves.

The manner in which Koestler develops Feya differs from his development of Rubashov significantly. Rubashov's personality was evidently a product of certain ideas that ordered his life. Feyda is a product of a combination of environmental influences and his psychological response to them. Whereas in Rubashov the interest was in his ideas, in Feyda, Koestler seems to have said everything he had to say about the commissar's ideas and turns instead to his psychology. In this it is the psychology of conversion that most interests him. Here Feyda is posed as the direct counterpart to Hydie. By setting the conversion of each alongside the other, their respective strengths and weaknesses can be more easily observed.

Feyda's conversion to a revolutionary ideology is not born of the strength of the idea. He inherited the idea of revolution from his family. It was a natural part of the very air he breathed as a child. His father and grandfather instilled in him the idea of "the Great Change" that he later identified with the party. It never occured to him that the future would hold anything else in store. Although the idea of the Great Change could be likened to a religious vision, formal religion was regarded as an ideology of the ruling class as the Great Change was of the working class. His illiterate grandfather had absorbed just enough of modern science to argue in behalf of the materialistic conception of creation. The old man conveyed to young Feyda a naive belief in the ability of science to solve all problems.[7] But with Feyda's childhood described as a flashback in the novel, there is a touch of irony in his vision of the future. In the late 1950s, the setting for the novel, the Great Change has become the Great Nightmare. Feyda can recall the fate of Rubashov even as he imagines the utopian future that never quite seems to come.

Feyda's conversion is seen as a product of his social environment more than as a deliberate choice among alternatives. Hydie, by way of contrast, was a religious convert for more intellectualized reasons. Nevertheless, Koestler portrays the conversion of the soul to religion as rooted in the same psychological phenomenon that under other circumstances can lead to politics. Both are built on a faith in certain abstract—that is, theoretical—ordering principles. Even though the objects of their faith may differ, it is a similar psychology that enables them to understand each other better than could an outsider to such faith. Feyda's illusions are, however, built on a nineteenth century science that is, despite its weaknesses, closer to the truth of things than is Hydie's medieval religion. When both are put to the political test, Feyda's Promethian vision proves stronger and more resiliant thay Hydie's God.

While other characters in the novel are faced with political choices at various stages, only Feyda has something that could be termed a class consciousness in Marxist terms. Because of his social origins, he is instinctively a revolutionary. Although in his maturity he has lost the original innocence of the time he first whole heartedly accepted the reality of the Great Change, he cannot think of the revolution as evil. His original faith never changed, and it enabled him to explain away the experienced incongruities between theory and practice in his maturity:

[Feyda] never lost his belief. He learned that the Change might come only gradually; that it would not fall from the sky, but had to be helped by man's endeavor, including his own; that to reach the ultimate goal, one might have to follow many detours and at times lose it even from sight. . . . But despite all those modifications, the belief in the Great Change remained the guiding star of all his thoughts, his conscience and other actions."[8]

What Feyda's faith does is to reconcile the law of detours with the Free Commonwealth. As Koestler explains away Feyda's present position in the party, it hardly seems that any other fate could possibly have awaited him. Even in his maturity, there is a childlike innocence in his faith as Koestler describes it. His objective cruelty is a guileless sort that does not make him any the less guilty but does tend to make the question of punishment pointless. How can someone be punished if he does not recognize his actions as wrong? Feyda sees his mission as "constructing the future," while Hydie's longing is for a decadant past.[9]

Koestler, however, does not allow Feyda's vision of the Great Change go unchallenged. In *The Age of Longing*, there is far less rational argument on behalf of the commissar than was the case in *Darkness at Noon*. Feyda's rationalism has led him to believe that he can predict the future with absolute certainty, given the correct stimulus. But when he attempts a demonstration on Hydie, it leads to his personal downfall. Her emotional response was wholly unanticipated, and he cannot account for it as Hydie does. Even in his maturity, there still is no room for a grammatical fiction.

Although the private scandal that follows from Hydie's attack sends Feyda off to Siberia, the party as a whole does not suffer. Even in exile, Feyda can hopefully await the time when he will be returned to the good graces of the party. The Russian invasion of France does not in the end turn on anything Feyda personally contributed, but is the result of a general weakening of the West.

III *Julien*

As with all of Koestler's novels, it is the clash of political ideas that is the matrix from which the situations evolve. This means that either an individual or a theoretical framework ties together the strands of thought. It is one of the organizational problems of *The Age of Longing* that no single idea or person provides unequivocally this reference point. Julien Delattre is the person who comes closest to filling this necessary role. Although Hydie and Feyda are more crucial to the novel as a whole, Julien is the link between them and a host of lesser figures. Without Julien, the novel would be torn apart by a welter of conflicting points of view, and Koestler's own understanding might be lost.

Julien is the leavening agent of common sense in the ideological arguments between the Free Commonwealth and the halfway house ideologies in the salons of Paris. There is a strong temptation to see in Julien a fictional creation by Koestler of himself. The two have much in common, and it is through the person of Julien that Koestler finds a spokesman for his own views in the novel. To the extent that Julien is a self-portrait, it is not an altogether flattering one, but it bears the unmistakable imprint of honesty in description.

Julien is a pessimist. He is an ex-member of the party who has now become one of its most implacable intellectual foes. As a young poet in the 1930s, he had been attracted to the party by a sense of idealism that he now finds embarrassing. Though he has renounced his political past, he is determined to learn from it. He continues to believe that he joined the party for the right reasons, and that to face the future realistically he must somehow find another outlet for the same reasons.[10]

Since he is unique among the Parisian intellectuals for having known the party from inside and out, he is convinced that he knows it better than anyone else. The experience has left him permanently scarred in politics, and he is treated as something of a political leper by those others who are still motivated by various ideologies. He says, "I take it for granted that one must fight in self-defense, and in defense of the minimum decencies of life, and so on. I merely wish to point out that this has nothing to do with . . . signposts and dialectics and with leftism, rightism, capitalism, and socialism or any other idea or ism. When I hear those words, I smell the sewers."[11] This sums up Koestler's own position perhaps as well as anything he wrote on politics. But his opposition to political ideologies makes him an outcast to others who still cling to them. This includes Hydie, whose sense of longing for something to believe in is repulsed by Julien's self-critical pessimism. As an outsider, Julien sees himself as something of a modern day Cassandra, trying to tell people what they ought to know already. He is obsessed with the threat posed by the Free Commonwealth to the point whereby it poisons every other interest and friendship. It makes others feel awkward and uncomfortable in his presence. He says of himself that he is likened to a "pox-ridden idealist who knows that he lives in a dying world but has no inkling of the new world which will replace it."[12] He is a dreary figure indeed, but he shares in common with Hydie one point; he has no fixed values, nothing to believe in. His sole motivating force seems to be an unending hostility toward the Free Commonwealth.

What most sets Julien apart from his contemporaries is his vision of the impending apocalypse and his eagerness to tell everyone about it. Europe is doomed, but only he and a handful of others can see it. Everyone else hides the truth they are afraid to openly admit, even to themselves. He is an unwanted prophet. In his self-appointed role as Cassandra, he has a single recurring nightmare: "Cassandra struck dumb at the critical moment. She hears her own warning shriek, but she alone hears it: no warning comes from her mouth."[13] Symbolically, Hydie is cast in the role of the one who does not hear the warning from Julien until the end when it may be too late.

The political struggle against the Free Commonwealth has exhausted Julien spiritually. He is worn out by what one character calls the "gangrene" that is killing Europe. In the final chapter, as rumors of Russian paratroopers landing in the outskirts of Paris spread, Julien is making his plans to join a new underground and fight them. But unlike the underground of World War II against the Nazis, when he knew why he fought, now his actions are reflexive, like the muscle spasms of a corpse. There is a vague optimism, similar to that of Peter in *Arrival and Departure,* that the future will be better, but it has an even more hollow ring than before. He says: "I have a hunch that the time is not far when a new spiritual ferment will arise, as spontaneous and irresistable as early Christianity or the Renaissance. But meanwhile, I have no program to offer."[14]

The one thing of which Julien is certain is that there will be no turning back to the old values of the past. God and Christianity are dead. Given a choice between a religion that promises an eternity in hell for one's sins or the Free Commonwealth that only promises thirty years in Siberia, Julien would unhesitatingly chose the latter.[15] This is not entirely because Julien is hostile to religion per se, although he is that, as much as it is a rejection of the past and the yogi ethic in politics. Julien is a humanist of the secular world. In politics, religion is a holdover from the past, and Julien is a futurist.

Julien is, in his own way, a man of science as much as Feyda. But in lieu of a deterministic science, Julien posits a relativistic science. The result is that he ends at a different point in politics than does Feyda. Julien longs for his lost idealism and the revolutionary faith of his younger days. In this he is much like the other characters. But unlike the others, his scientific reason tells him that such naive idealism is an illusion. He says to Father Millet: "believe me that I envy with all my heart those colleagues of my craft and generation who, in middle age, acquire the true faith as others acquire ulcers."[16] But faith is not reason and Julien cannot abandon what he sees as the rational course of searching for a god that will not fail as had revolution and the God of the desert. Julien sums up his current belief in the aphorism, "To comprehend everything, to forgive nothing."[17] It is, as Julien is told, a hard and perhaps arrogant creed. He accepts that judgement as valid enough and as the particular cross he must bear in life; "the maxim solves several hoary dilemmas implicit in the human condition." Exactly what those dilemmas may be is never made explicit. But from the general understanding of the dilemmas in political life as Koestler has previously drawn them, it would appear to be on the order of a compromise between the yogi and the commissar. Julien sees himself as a realist and a pragmatist. Such pessimistic realism is the only viable halfway house in the modern world in which the new scientific world is still in the process of becoming. Reason defined exclusively in terms of the yogi and the commissar seems to have broken down in *The Age of Longing*. Julien is a solitary figure, perhaps indicative of the intellectual of the interregnum, who makes himself the judge of right and wrong independent of parties and priests.

IV   *"Witches' Sabbath"*

Interwoven with the major dialogues and characters of *The Age of Longing* are a host of lesser figures and minor dialogues. Within the novel there is a particularly acid-tongued subplot in which Koestler finds the authors' ultimate revenge upon his critics—a parody on them one and all. Appropriately enough, it is Julien who leads Hydie, and with her the reader as well, into the murky corners of Parisian intellectual life. He serves as an interlocutor between Hydie and a satarized form of Koestler's critics that is one of the high points of the novel.

By the time *The Age of Longing* appeared in 1951, Koestler had built up an especially voiciferous following of vehement critics. For the most part, they were intellectuals who had been fellow travelers or party members during the 1930s but, unlike Koestler, felt no sense of shame for having supported Stalin at that time. And among many who did feel a sense of guilt, Koestlers's constant harping on that guilt, never allowing them to ignore their own past, did little to endear him to them. Perhaps the best known critics were Jean Paul Sartre and Maurice Merleau-Ponty, founders of *Les Temps Modernes*, the major Left newspaper in Paris at that time. Maurice Merleau-Ponty's *Humanism and Terror*, a passionate critique of

Darkness at Noon and defense of Stalin's purge trials, had appeared in 1947 and was still a fresh item of debate among intellectuals. Koestler was anxious to strike back.

Koestler extracted his literary revenge on his tormenters, much as Dante had done, through a series of biting portraits placing his worst enemies in a modern hell. The modern hell, in contrast with that of Dante, is "most respectable and civilized." It has a moderate degree of order, is slightly stuffy, and is extremely pretentious in its own supposed ability to understand the nature of things. It is a place populated chiefly with intellectual prostitutes who are prepared to defend every action of the Free Commonwealth and to be equally critical of every action by the West to defend itself. Their terms of political discourse seem borrowed from the "newspeak" so graphically described by George Orwell in *Nineteen Eighty-Four.* Julien calls such distortions at their intellectual gathering places a "witches' sabbath." It is an ironical twist to the surface respectability of these modern sophists. They don't believe in witches, and yet they are under the spell of a demonic ideology. "Most of the people here do not know they are bewitched," Julien says to Hydie at one of their meetings, and if you tried to tell them otherwise, "[they] would think you are mad because there is no witchcraft in the twentieth century."[18]

Witchcraft of the ideological sort plays an integral part in the conversion to the commissars' revolution. What Julien means, aside from the obvious pleasure Koestler takes in such comments for their own sake, is that the party ideology is like a witch's spell. That spell first destroys critical faculties of the mind and then leaves the body to a Pavlovian interpretation, such as that of Feyda, of stimulus and response. When critical reason is destroyed by political ideologies, all that is left is a mechanistic science of the commissar's world.

Attending the witches' sabbath, in addition to Julien and Hydie, are most of Koestler's foes. Sartre, for example, is recreated in the form of the pompous Professor Pontieux; "a Professor of Philosophy. He can prove everything he believes and believes everything he can prove."[19] At the end of the novel he is arrested by the police, just as the invasion by the Free Commonwealth is beginning. Julien dismisses his arrest with a cavalier shrug, saying, "He was just a clever imbecile. . . . It wasn't his fault if people took him seriously."[20]

In many respects, the case could be made that the witches' sabbath could be taken as *the* theme of the novel. This would be an exaggeration, but there is much to recommend it. It is the intellectual revolutionary, the blind supporter of the Free Commonwealth, who comes in for Koestler's greatest scorn. Professor Pontieux is the perfect symbol of this contemptible lot. The intellectuals are all theory in their conception of political reality and live as far from the world of practical consequences of their theories as one could imagine. Collectively they represent the rupture between theory and practice that enables them to rationalize the barbarism of the Free Commonwealth and to ignore a moral dimension in its actions. Mesmerized by their own sophistry, they have nevertheless managed to carry along with them large numbers of confused and bewildered ordinary citizens. They live a life ordered around trite slogans and aphorisms of the age. It is characteristic of the time that these cliches are treated as profound insights into the dilemma of the human condition. If a new god is about to be born, it will have to be a god of new science and not one that comes from the dominant modes of thought found among the professors of philosophy.

CHAPTER 7

The Science of the Mind

FOLLOWING the publication of his impressive two volume autobiography in 1954, Arthur Koestler seemed to bid farewell to his preoccupation with the dilemma of revolution in the modern world. His subsequent writing reflected his long-standing interest in science, which predated his party affiliations. As a student in Vienna, he had majored in science at the university. His early newspaper days with the Ullstein chain in Germany had brought him to the position of science editor. But this apparent reawakening of interest in science was neither sudden nor without signs in his political fiction. By the time *The Age of Longing* appeared in 1951, it was evident that Koestler was searching for the rational structure of knowledge that informed the dilemma of political choices. The idea of the yogi and the commissar, revealing though it had been, proved insufficient by itself to account for the full range of political dilemmas in the twentieth century. Koestler was inexorably led back to the conflicting notions of science that informed opinion in the twentieth century. Rather than viewing his scientific writing as a new direction to his work, it is more accurate to see in it the logical extension of his political fiction. Because certain problems arose in his treatment of political choice that pointed toward a failure of theory, he began to consider the problem of knowledge as central to an inquiry into the contemporary human condition. Because the problem of knowledge seemed to him to be a scientific one, a fictional exploration of it did not seem in order.

The failure of politics in the modern world, in Koestler's view, was seen as a failure of theory. In turn, that failure of theory was linked to an outmoded notion of deterministic science that carried over from the nineteenth century. It was a materialistic science of the mind that ultimately needed to be combated in order to restore science, properly understood in light of recent developments, to a rational position in the human condition. A new, nondeterministic, nonmaterial science of the mind was the first order of business in the restoration of reason to politics. The ruptured connection between thought and action that had occured in the past was the impetus for Koestler's exploration of science. The structure of modern science for Koestler is a probabilistic one. With a collapse of the older, deterministic understanding of science comes the collapse of those political theories, such as Marxism, that rest on those scientific assumptions. Marxism and the commissar have lost their claim to be founded on science in the contemporary world. Yet their political prescriptions persist, Koestler maintains, because there is no other widely accepted answer to the dilemmas of the human condition that unite theory and practice into a single paradigm. It gives to revolutionary theories the appearance of scientific rationality that is missing from their critics, such as Koestler. But this appearance of rationality is an illusion according to Koestler. It is based on a science of the mind that is becoming more antiquated and anachronistic with each passing decade of the twentieth century. But the dilemma of the commissar's science suggests the remedy for its own defects. The restoration of a true science of the mind must be an inquiry into the science of the mind conducted in the light of the most recent advances.

In his autobiography, Koestler had attributed to his early scientific education certain habits of mind that eventually led to his break with the Communist party. Chief among them, he said, was a sense of intellectual modesty that rejected the "total explanations" offered by Marxists.[1] During his days in the party, he had managed to submerge his concern with what he called "the crisis of determinism." But eventually he broke with the party on the issue of determinism in political actions. Here his recollections seem to be accurate. For example, where Marx had argued for a class structure of knowlege, Koestler had always insisted that scientific truths, whatever they might be, are independent of the social structure of society. The social structure enters the picture at the point where science is applied—in actions, but not in the ideas themselves. This is a difference that is worth noting. It places Koestler well outside the Marxist scheme of ideas, a point often overlooked by those critics who have claimed at times that he remained a theoretical Marxist even while rejectiing its more sordid practices.

Koestler's study of the science of the mind was in the form of a trilogy on that science—*The Sleepwalkers, The Act of Creation,* and

The Ghost in the Machine. In addition to these major works, there were several lesser, more specialized studies on various tangents that also form a part of the overall picture—*The Case of the Mid-Wife Toad, The Challenge of Chance,* and *The Roots of Coincidence*. The range of subjects covered includes biology, genetics, extrasensory perception, and the history of modern science. But is spite of their incredible diversity of subject matter, they all point to a single problem: the structure of reason necessary to understand the human mind scientifically.

I   The Sleepwalkers

By far the most impressive and most influential of the major works on the science of the mind was *The Sleepwalkers,* which appeared in 1959. It is a survey of scientific thought from the time of the ancient Greeks through the Newtonian revolution. The principle emphasis, however, is on the period from the time of Copernicus through Galileo. The history is notable for several reasons. First of all, it must be counted among the half dozen or so works on the history of science in the post war period that helped to change opinions on the shape of that history. It challenged previous assumptions about the nature of the scientific enterprise that were not altogether welcome.

What *The Sleepwalkers* challenged was the conception of science as a discipline emerging from a tradition of previous superstition along a linear dimension of history where pure reason triumphs over ignorance. It is a critique of the progressivist interpretation of history that tied science to a Newtonian universe of determinism and materialism. His argument is that science is not progressive in character, that there is no clear boundary between knowledge and superstition in science, and that instead of traveling a straight line into the twentieth century it follows "a wild zig-zag which alternates between progress and disaster."[2]

Koestler was not the first historian of modern science to make these assertions. The introduction to *The Sleepwalkers* is by Herbert Butterfield, who had said much the same thing in 1949, in his important study, *The Origins of Modern Science*. Furthermore, E. A. Burtt's *The Metaphysical Foundations of Modern Physical Science* had hinted at the same argument in 1924. But Koestler's work had an impact beyond these and other studies for at least two important reasons, one of which may be attributed to the design of the work and the other quite accidental to it. The first is due to Koestler's lengthy and controversial treatment of Johannes Kepler, which is for all practical purposes a book within a book. Indeed, Koestler later published the section on Kepler as a separate title, *The Watershed*. But the other, and perhaps most important, factor that contributed to the impact of the work was the appearance three years later of Thomas Kuhn's profoundly influential *The Structure of Scientific Revolutions*. On the basis of wholly independent research, Kuhn had developed a remarkably similar thesis. In retrospect, the publication of Kuhn's study has tended to give Koestler's work the appearance of phophecy with regard to this increasingly persuasive perspective on the history of science. Despite some flaws in research and argument, *The Sleepwalkers* has stood up better as an interpretation of scientific creativity and development than have many of the contemporary arguments against it by progressivist critics.

Koestler's interpretation of the roots of scientific creativity through the detailed study of Kepler forms the cornerstone of his argument. In his minute re-creation of the mind of Kepler, Koestler recreates his own understanding of scientific creativity. His basic argument is that the act of creation is itself a mysterious process about which nothing can be known in terms of origins. All we can do is to observe the act as it works itself out in the mind of the scientist and as he imperfectly translates that process into something to be comprehended by outsiders. Most of ordinary science is simply the reasoned verification of truths that do not seem to have their origin in reason—certainly not the mechanistic conception of reason that people have tended to attribute to a Newtonian world view.

The importance of Kepler in Koestler's scheme of things is due to the quasi-mystical basis of Kepler's version of science and to Koestler's own affinity for the occult in human affairs. In the selection of Kepler as a symbol of creativity, Koestler had no need to justify that choice; there is no doubt that Kepler stands as one of the giants in Western thought who has altered our cosmological view of the nature of things. But what most startled many in Koestler's version of Kepler was his presentation of the development of his science. After a close reading of Kepler's own writings, Koestler denied that this was a classic case of pure reason overcoming past superstition. In Koestler's version, Kepler is as firmly rooted in the past as in the bold new future of science. He looked upon science as an extension of questions that the modern world would understand as occult in origin. Furthermore, and even more of a scandal to progressivist historians, the primary opposition to Kepler's revolutionary discoveries in astronomy did not come from priests and other supposed forces of darkness, but from his fellow scientists. It was Galileo, for example, who ridiculed Kepler's theory that the rise and fall of the tides was somehow connected with the moon. The notion that the scientific community itself could sometimes stand athwart the progress of the mind was to many the most objectionable feature of *The Sleepwalkers*.

In what might be called the "liberal" interpretation of Renaissance science, the triumph of the scientific view of Copernicus, Kepler, and Galileo symbolized the triumph of reason over ignorance. But to Koestler it symbolized even more a genuine tragedy, the full effects of which have only become apparent in the twentieth century. The triumph of science also meant what he termed "the parting of the ways" between scientific reason and moraltiy. Science came to be associated increasingly with the deterministic model that is the cornerstone of the commissar's world view. Morality, on the other hand, has ever since tended to become an abstract and disembodied spirit, unable to rationally calculate the relationship between ends and means. This parting of the ways is the watershed of modern thought in Koestler's view. To rejoin these two strands—reason with morality—is thus understood as the great task of the rational reconstruction of the human condition in the twentieth century.

It is significant to note that the first place Koestler began his exploration of the science of the mind was with its history. He had always acknowledged that a particular philosophy of history was implicit in the respective positions of the yogi and the commissar. But here Koestler expands his earlier views to argue that a rational praxis of politics cannot be established until it first deals with the question of when and why the commissar's view came to prevail in the modern world. Previously he had suggested certain of the broad outlines of this approach but had never really developed their implications. In *Arrival and Departure*, for example, he had asked the question of how is it that an irrational past can shape actions in the present. Peter's cure was at least partly affected by an inquiry into the origins of his illness. What emerges from *The Sleepwalkers* is the notion that one of the most crucial functions of reason is the illumination of where reason has gone astray.

It does not follow from this analysis, however, that Koestler believes that twentieth century science can become rational in the commissar's sense of rationalism. Science is always linked, at least at its most creative point, with a sort of chaotic mysticism that prevents a final perfection of reason. In his autobiography, he had spoken of a "two-front war" that he constantly waged against both materialism and religious faith.[3] True science he interpreted to be a path between these to extremes. As a former member of the Communist party, he was always keenly aware of the power of faith. But after his break, he was especially sensitive to any tendencies in that direction. His own vision of scientific reason was understood by him to be at odds with both the yogi and the commissar.

His conception of scientific reality was built around a hierarchial concept with three interlocking components. Science was to play a role in each of these three levels of reality, but was never wholly a part of any of them. The first order of this reality was the lowest level of sensory perception that is entirely materialistic. The commissar accurately perceives this dimension of reality. But such materialism is incomplete because it cannot be ordered without some reference to the second order of reality, which Koestler defines as the conceptual framework by which the senses are interpreted. This framework is not itself accessible to sensory perception. In its turn, this second level gives way to the third and highest level, which gives form to the second. This third level is one that Koestler frankly calls "occult."[4] Science, properly understood in Koestler's view, is the integration of these three orders or levels of reality. They are ordered by a reason that stands apart from them and at the same time cannot be understood except by reference to these levels. Koestler likens it to the idea of the Holy Trinity in Christian thought where he admits to having borrowed this conceptual framework. The view of science that emerges from *The Sleepwalkers* is essentially an elaboration upon an idea that Koestler appears to have worked out at the same time he was writing his fiction in the early 1940's.

The science of *The Sleepwalkers* is not viewed as the progressive salvation of mankind but rather has a tragic side not usually described by most historians of science. It is the divorce of science from morality in the period roughly from Copernicus to Newton. The tragedy was not the spiteful work of narrow-minded churchmen: "Throughout the golden age of humanism. . .the scientists remained the sacred cows of cardinals and popes."[5] The famous trial of Galileo for his scientific discoveries, "the greatest scandal in Christendom," Koestler concludes was due more to an unfortunate blend of personalities, including that of Galileo himself, than anything esle. The confrontation between Galileo and the church was, at any rate, an aberration and not typical of the usually harmonious relationship between science and theology. The reason why the two parted ways in

Koestler's account is far different from the conventional one of scientific truth battling superstitious dogma. It was in the nature of the materialistic view of the universe that the two visions should eventually follow separate paths into the twentieth century: "The mechanical universe could accommodate no transcendental factor. Theology and physics parted ways not in anger, but in sorrow, not because of Signor Galileo, but because they became bored with and had nothing more to say to each other."[6]

Such a split approaches an explanation of why the yogi and the commissar are the opposing symbols of reality in the twentieth century. It places the split more recently in time than *The Gladiators*, but that novel had never been intended as historical fiction in the first place; it was always an allegorical representation of a predicament of the human condition that was a fact of modern life as much as of ancient life. Although this separation was "without hostility or drama," it is all the more politically dangerous because of the absence of hostility. The perception of the estrangement by scientists and humanists is real enough, but to Koestler there is a profound misunderstanding on both sides as to the causes and consequences of that separation. As long as materialism has held the scientific fort against countervailing theories, morality and science could not even talk to one another, because they each spoke a wholly different language.

In spite of the history of the split, *The Sleepwalkers* is a more optimistic work than some of Koestler's other writing. The twentieth century offers an opportunity to heal that centuries old break. The materialist universe has suddenly and dramatically collapsed under the impact of relativity. In political theories, however, there is a lag in the ability to apply the new science to ideas about the polity. The consequence is a paradox; the progress of scientific reason is in inverse ratio to the ability of statesmen to use it. The gap between the two is the measure of irrationality. A real dialogue between the two poles is possible, but since it requires a choice on both parts to engage in that dialogue Koestler is not entirely certain that it will actually take place. *The Call-Girls*, which appeared in 1972, may be seen as a more pessimistic view of the breakdown of a possible dialogue between science and humanism.

In questioning the notion of progress in science, Koestler anticipated similar arguments advanced a few years later by Thomas Kuhn in his *The Structure of Scientific Revolutions*. The apparant coincidence between the two helped Koestler considerably in that he was not merely an eccentric but had helped to stake out an increasingly powerful position. Instead of progress, science follows a zig-zag course, and what is considered "scientific" at any given point along its path is very much dependent upon the prevailing consensus of opinion. The new consensus is as revolutionary as Newton, but the effects of that revolution are only dimly perceived, if at all, by the affected communities. The progress of science is not matched by a corresponding increase in the evolution of man's mind to cope with these changes. "Progress can by definition never go wrong; evolution constatly does; and so does the evolution of ideas, including those of the 'exact sciences.' "[7]

What Koestler confronts the reader with in *The Sleepwalkers* is the view of evolution gone haywire. Man's mind is simply unable to keep up with or comprehend the explosion of knowledge in science. It poses a dilemma that goes deeper than that of the yogi and the commissar—the prospect, in Koestler's view, that the species of man may not be able to survive unless the evolutionary process is directed by reason rather than by chance. What he implicitly argues is the notion that the split between science and morality may be a consequence of the imperfect evolution of the mind as much as of historical chance. But if we can know the defects of the species, he argues, it may be possible to correct them. A crucial question for Koestler then becomes understanding what is meant by evolution.

Koestler defines evolution as "differentiation of structure and integration of function." What this means is that as the parts of an organism become increasingly specialized, the more elaborate must be the coordination between them. Here biological evolution parallels society, and an understanding of science can contribute to political theory. Modern society has become a highly specialized and differentiated organism. Yet political activity, the means by which these parts are coordinated, is dominated by outmoded concepts of science. The inability of politics to integrate the functions of modern society are evidence of social and biological evolution off track. The biological failure is in the inability of Nature to evolve man's mind to a point whereby it can cast-off self-destructive urges and harmonize these diverse parts of society. The result is the political neurosis of a Peter in the inability to link together scientific reasoning about politics with its practice; "In a house divided, both inhabitants lead a thwarted existence."[8] Values demand a hierarchial structure arranged in a serial order as the precedence. The dilemma for Koestler at this point is that there is no apparant hierarchy in post-Newtonian science. To go beyond the obstacle of the erratic evolution of man's mind in Nature, establish a notion of hierarchy compatable with modern science, and apply this reason to man's social condition through politics was the problem of Koestler's next two works on the science of the mind.

II *Science and the Restoration of Values*

The Sleepwalkers had analysed and defined the nature of the modern dilemma of the human condition deeper than the problem of the yogi and the commissar. But it did not really point to a way out of the predicament. *The Act of Creation* and *The Ghost in the Machine,* which completed the trilogy on the science of the mind, sought to answer that problem. Between them they established Koestler's conception of the hierarchy both of biological science and of social values and gave his prescription for a solution to the predicament of the human condition in the twentieth century.

At one level, *The Act of Creation* is an encyclopedia of Koestler's interests in science. It is the longest of all his works and in many respects the most difficult. It is an attempt to explain what he readily conceeds may be unexplainable—the nature of human creativity. From his reading of Kepler as well as his own introspective questioning, he had come to see the creative act as something shrouded in mystery. He begins the study with an impressive inquiry into a variety of creative acts: humor, wisdom, poetry, art, and finally, creative writing. These are in turn placed within a larger framework of habit and originality. Most especially Koestler was concerned with how scientific creativity broke with prior molds of thought and how much of those prior patterns of thought it retained. The two aspects of the work that are most pertinent here are those sections dealing with hierarchies in the act of creation and with his criticism of behavioral psychology.

The concept of hierarchy, as Koestler develops the term, abandons the concept of a serial order of precedence. Such a concept, he argues, is no longer applicable in the world of modern science. Instead, hierarchy means a specialized type of organization, such as the military, in which overall control is highly centralized while subordinate units are left with a large measure of autonomy even as they are integrated into the whole.[9] All advance forms of social organization, he says, are hierarchic along these lines; the individual is part of the family, the family is part of the community, the community is part of the nation, and so forth. The same pattern also holds for biological organisms. Even in the individual, there is the same analagous relationship between simple and complex skills. "The single individual represents the top-level of the organismic hierarchy and at the same time the lowest unit of the social hierarchy."[10] The social wholes—such as family, community—are held together politically by a complex ordering of laws, customs, habits, and what we generally call values. The control of these social subunits, unlike biological subunits, is very much dependent upon the willingness of the individuals who compose them to voluntarily abide by these established forms of organizational control. When tensions arise between these parts and the larger wholes, one or both may become "excited" and the system is "out of control." Social cohesion is threatened, and hence arises the dilemma of the human condition, symbolized in his earlier writing by the yogi and the commissar but essentially unchanged later.

What happens in Koestler's conception of hierarchy is that the terms "whole" and "part" lose any absolute significance. The terms express a relativistic relationship to things larger or smaller, but no whole or part can be said to be an end in itself. It is a mysterious process by which the creative act is linked through the mind to the observable end products. The association between mind and act is what he calls "bisociates." It is essentially an elaboration of an idea Koestler had earlier stated in his essay "The Yogi and the Commissar (II)," written in 1944:

The laws of the higher cannot be reduced to, nor predicted from the lower level;
the phenomenon of the lower level and their laws are implied in the higher level, but
the phenomenon of the higher order if manifest on the lower level appear as unexplainable and miraculous.[11]

Perhaps one of the most interesting aspects of this view of scientific hierarchy is that Koestler understood it to be identical with the basic structure of Christian thought. Yet Koestler never saw it as a religious notion. It was simply the structure of the objective order of things, and religion has nothing to do with it except that some religious writers had expressed it better than others. But whereas the religious understanding had pointed toward an explicit teleology of human existence, Koestler stopped short of this assertion. In Koestler's conception of the mind, thought progresses from the relatively simple to the relatively complex. There would seem to be an implied end, a highest good perhaps, of this process, but there is not.

Koestler's hierarchy is one without an apex. When *The Act of Creation* first appeared, this absence of an apex in a hierarchial system encountered some justifiable criticism.[12] Koestler sought to answer this criticism in *The Ghost in the Machine* with a discussion of what he called "holons" that at least served to clarify his own position, though it did not completely satisfy all of his critics.

What *The Act of Creation* says to the reader is that there is emerging in the twentieth century a rational science of the mind. The difficulty, however, is that this science of the mind does not have a unified theory in the sense of a consensus paradigm in the scientific community. Its basic components are still scattered throughout the laboratories of the modern world and have yet to be assembled. What is need, Koestler implicitly argues, is a single, commonly accepted paradigm, much like the idea of evolution in biology, that will bring the diverse strands together into a whole cloth. Once the paradigm of the mind has been agreed upon, the link between it and the political world will at least be made easier. It is the only rational basis for a political praxis available in the latter half of the twentieth century. The result should be a more rational basis for political action. Political acts are themselves a part of the creative process and follow as a reflection of the theories behind them; they are more or less reasonable in direct relationship to the rationality of the theory. The potential for a new, truly scientific praxis is one of the unique features of the present time. But it is only that—"potential"—unless one acts politically to realize it.

III   The Ghost in the Machine

Koestler's third volume in his science of the mind, *The Ghost in the Machine*, is less tightly organized than the first two. But what it lacks in organization is at least partly made up for in the force and clarity of his basic points. The work is specifically intended to tie together the remaining loose ends of the previous argument. In addition, it may be seen as Koestler's defense of the grammatical fiction in the language of science rather than the language of politics.

A major portion of *The Ghost in the Machine* is given over to Koestler's long-standing attack on behavioral psychology.

An age is drawing to a close in the history of psychology: the age of the dehumanization of man. Words like "purpose", "volition", "introspection", "consciousness", "insight", words which used to be banned as obscene from the vocabulary of the so-called "Behavioral Sciences", are triumphantly reasserting themselves—not as abstract philosophical concepts, but as indispensible descriptive tools without which even a rat's actions in an experimental maze do not make sense.[13]

The difficulty with behavioral psychology, in Koestler's view, is that it now stands in the way of a more scientific conception of the mind. The outmoded language of materialism obfuscates rather than clarifies the problem of the human condition. This results not only in a distortion of the phenomenon described as it is verbalized, but also in an inability to rationally integrate the findings into a truly scientific hierarchy. The behaviorists are still at what he has called the first level of reality; the strictly materialist level of comprehension.

In contrast to the determinism of the behaviorist, Koestler argues for a probabilistic understanding of science of the mind that is decidedly nondeterminist. It is also a science of hierarchies as he has used the term. The conception of hierarchy without an apex that was begun in *The Act of Creation* was completed in *The Ghost in the Machine*. To symbolize his refinements of such a hierarchy, he coined the term "holon"—from the Greek word *holos,* meaning whole, with the suffix *on,* which suggests a particle or a part. It is his basis for a relativistic conception of science that avoids the tendency toward moral irresponsibility that is the usual concomitant of relativism.

Taking up where he left off in *The Act of Creation,* Koestler begins his defense of his particular view of science by stating that wherever there is life it must be hierarchially organized. But, he goes on to say, "the first and universal characteristic of hierarchies is the relativity, and indeed ambiguity, of the terms 'part' and 'whole' when applied to sub-assemblies."[14] Neither wholes or parts exist in any absolute sense; every unit of analysis is at once a part as well as a whole of something else. In the absence of any genuine, knowable whole, there can be no true apex. "The members of a hierarchy, like the Roman god Janus, all have two faces looking in opposite directions."[15] This "Janus effect" is the fundamental feature of holons. In this description, what Koestler is trying to do is give to the notion of hierarchy and the relation of theory to practice in politics an entirely new paradigmatic structure.

Koestler is quite explicit in linking scientific holons to a new understanding of politics and theories of politics. All aspects of the human condition, he argues, can be understood in terms of these holons: biology, psychology, language, society, politics, etc. Social organization is rational whenever the subunits are in accord with one another as well as the next higher level. For example, when language describes social hierarchies truthfully, we may say that it is theoretically rational. On the other hand, whenever the political language we use does not describe a hierachial organization, it may be presumed that the language, and hence the theory, is irrational. The consequence of this irrationality will be the politics of either the yogi or the commissar.

Complex societies are structured by numerous types of interlocking hierarchies—economic, legal, family, religious, etc. Historically, social organizations in the state could always be described, more or less, by analogous references to holons until the dawn of the modern era. The breakdown of these social hierarchies working harmoniously with one another came in the wake of the scientific revolution of Copernicus, Kepler, Galileo, Newton, and others. In the modern world, new towns and cities have grown up that are better described by references to an atomistic model—an excessive individualism with no evident cohesion or hierarchic structure that typifies the normal pattern of social holons. It is evidence of society in disarray. The conclusion Koestler draws from this analysis is that modern society is irrationally ordered and that the very language of the social sciences, which ought to describe reality, distorts the nature of things. Unless the language is changed to reflect the underlying reality there can be no way out of the predicament.

"No man is an island," Koestler writes, "he is a holon."[16] But the individual experiences his own individuality in the form of a self-assertive tendency against the larger groups of which he is but a part. There is thus a natural, built-in antagonism between a natural individualism and an equally natural tendency toward integration into larger groupings. When the integrative impulse is too strong, the individual loses his personality, such as in the case of Rubashov. When the self-assertive aspect is too strong it can tear society apart. The political record of the twentieth century suggests that we are living in a period when the self-assertive tendencies are out of control.[17] The social holons are not arranged the way they should be. The reaction of the commissars is the logical consequence of the breakdown of social holons.

The theme of evolution gone amuck had been hinted at as early as *The Gladiators:* "God created the world in five days, and He was in too much of a hurry. Many things went wrong in all this hurry, and when he arrived at the making of man, on the sixth day, He was irritable and tired perhaps."[18] But when the Essene spoke these words in the 1939 novel, Koestler had no solution to the problem. What distinguishes, *The Ghost in the Machine* from his earlier fiction is that by the 1960s Koestler had a proposal that he hoped would correct the defects of evolution in nature. Basically, his solution for the problem of evolution is for man, through science, to take over the direction of his own future. It is an essentially Promethian act: "I would prefer to set my hopes on moral persuasion by word and example. But we are a mentally sick race, and as such deaf to persuasion. . . .Nature has let us down. . .and time is running out."[19]

Koestler's proposal for modern science to take over the direction of future evolution of the human species is both necessary for the survival of the race and possible because of recent scientific breakthroughs. Men cannot expect, he says, to witness in the foreseeable future those necessary changes in human nature by the normal, undirected evolutionary process that will serve the purpose of survival. Biological evolution seems to him to have ceased with the Cro-Magnon epoch, and future changes in the species will have to be artificially (i.e., "scientifically") induced.[20] Objections will no doubt be raised, he notes, as to "who" will actually be in charge of making the necessary mutations. But these objections are to be overcome by the proper education, the basic purpose of which will be to inform people of the dangers of not acting. Science has reached a stage in the twentieth century in which the mechanics of biological evolution can be replicated in the laboratory: "We can only hope to survive as a species by developing techniques which supplant biological evolution."[21]

Where evolution has most noticably gone wrong is in the area of the brain of man. It is the task of the new science of the brain—or perhaps more accurately the science of the mind—to correct evolutionary deficiencies. This is what makes the science of the mind so critical and why its study now must take precedence over the study of politics, which is now seen as the study of the outward manifestations of a far deeper problem. The dilemmas of the yogi and the commissar are still real enough, but they are now symptoms of the problem and not the problem per se.

Specifically, Koestler proposed in *The Ghost in the Machine* that chemistry would come to rescue man from his neurotic impulse toward self-destruction. He suggested the introduction of pills that would create in the individual "a state of dynamic equilibrium in which thought and emotion are reunited and hierarchic order is restored."[22] The pills were not to be forced upon anyone, but their beneficial results would be so obvious that he found it difficult to believe anyone would not want them.[23] Indeed, their obvious benefits may obviate the need to educate the public as to their value. The pills would reduce conflict and bring thought and action back into harmony. Such a radically transformed human condition could be a new "Star of Bethlehem." It is a proposal based on the assumption that the modern dilemma of the human condition is only superficially expressed in politics, that its true origins go back to disorders of the mind, and that only science can properly treat the problem. It is, however, a view that does not represent a radical break with Koestler's earlier writing, but is a slightly different echo of *The Gladiators* and *Darkness at Noon*.

What Koestler hopes to achieve through this solution is not the attainment of any higher good in the classical sense of the term. He would claim that his aims are more modest—the survival of the human race. What he does not make clear is how this future would differ in the end from that proposed by Gletkin or Feyda, for example. The ultimate result of his analysis of the science of the mind is to cast the latter stages of his political thought in a definite Hobbesian mold. That is, the nature of political society is to be understood as the avoidance of evil rather than the pursuit of a good. Indeed, given Koestler's conception of holons and hierarchy, there is no place in Koestler's thought for a highest good, since that would imply an apex in a conception of hierarchy that is radically different from his own. The value of hierarchy, therefore, is essentially a negative value. That is, its chief value is tautologically defined as the elimination of conflict. But the elimination of conflict is seen by him as an end in itself that can and must be attained: "Aggression is not beyond our reach to correct. . . . Any condition that can be expressed in psychological terms should be accessible to psychological remedies. I don't think it is Utopian at all to hope that out of our laboratories will come a breakthrough."[24]

IV   *The God That Must Not Fail*

Taken together, Koestler's trilogy on the science of the mind and his lesser essays on science during the 1960s and 1970s suggest that science, properly understood, is the last line of rational existence to an otherwise chaotic and perhaps even demonic universe. Since politics by itself cannot hope to provide the cure to the dilemma of the yogi and the commissar, science must fill the void. Only science has sufficient authority in the modern world to deal with the dilemmas of the human condition.

There is an irony in Koestler's position in his science of the mind. In this phase of his writing, it is the scientist who steps forward to replace the commissar as the chief advocate of the notion that the end will justify the means. But at the same time, Koestler seems to have accepted one part of the yogi's position which he earlier questioned—that there can be no change in the human condition until there is a change in man's soul. That such a change is now brought about by chemistry rather than by religious conversion is less significant than the locus for the change itself. The notion that only a change in man's psyche can change society is the position Koestler earlier associated with the yogi. But at the same time, Koestler seems prepared to accept the means of the commissar to reach that end. Despite his disclaimers to the contrary, it is difficult to see how his pills could really be introduced except by some measure of coercion. Furthermore, as perhaps a final irony, Arthur Gilbert has pointed out in this connection that as the pills reduce conflict they have a built-in bias against any changes in the existing social order. It is as if this revolutionary change in human nature obviated the need for revolutionary political change.[25]

Koestler himself does not see the society that would emerge from the adoption of these pills as intrinsically status quo oriented. On the contrary, he sees his proposal as the advocacy of nonviolent change. It is a scientific defense of the grammatical fiction. It is the only way man's dignity can be defended, according to Koestler, because of the irrationality of the species. Something must be done to make him rational before mankind destroys itself. His is a reflection of a growing apprehension in his work that an irrational nature has produced an irrational man. It results in a feeling that reason will not prevail in human affairs until the very nature of man has been altered in both its psychological and biological foundations. In his essay on capital punishment, he wrote: "Deep inside every civilized being there lurks a tiny Stone Age man, dangling a club to rob and rape, and screaming an eye for an eye."[26]

What Koestler finds in his reading of modern science, especially those sciences concerned with human behavior, is that those things that call disorders out of habit in fact have a chemical origin. Certain types of mental disorders, previously intractable psychoses, even some forms of schizophrenia, he believes, have a biochemical base.[27]

This in turn reinforces his long-standing critique of behaviorism. Not because they are wholly wrong, since they can in fact alter individual behavior, but because, in addition to their value relativism, they cannot be applied on a mass scale; they require individual, one-on-one treatment. Psychoanalysis has, in his words, become "the therapy of the leisure class." Useful though it is in certain individual case, Western civilization as a whole is so far diseased that it is in need of some form of mass alteration of behavior patterns. Pills, because they can be used on a large scale, seem to be the most practical approach. Their use on such a scale would, he argues, amount to a reaffirmation of traditional values, albeit on a somewhat selective basis.

Regardless of criticism over specifics, there seems to be little doubt that Koestler sees his proposals as the scientific approach to the political dilemma of the human condition first set forth in his fiction. It is the way out of the problem of choice between the yogi and the commissar. If there is a change of mood between the former and the latter, it is in a sense that in science he is on the right theoretical track whereas in politics there was more uncertainty. The irrationality of the commissar is even more based on scientific irrationality in his later work than when the conceptualization was first formulated. Twentieth century science is light years away from the scientific world of Marx and the commissar, but the political world is remarkably similar. When Koestler returned to fiction in *The Call Girls*, following his science of the mind trilogy, it was with a keen awareness that politics was still his nemesis. Rational theory still could not make headway against irrational politics.

CHAPTER 8

A School for Cassandras

WHEN Arthur Koestler returned to writing fiction in 1972 with *The Call-Girls*, it was a significant work in several respects. First, it was undoubtedly his best fiction since *Darkness at Noon.* Second, it was his attempt to link his work in a science of the mind to its political applicability. It brought him back face to face with the vexing dilemma of ends and means in politics, but armed now with new theoretical conceptions of the problem that cast the dilemma of the yogi and the commissar in a different light. The strength of the novel is in Koestler's firm grasp of the scientific ideas involved and in his rich display of personalities attached to the various ideas. The discussion of ideas, which is a hallmark of Koestler's fiction, is here scientific ideas in a political context. In *The Call-Girls* it is the theoretical structure of modern science that overshadows political ideologies. But it is not a wholly rational science, merely one that is striving to become rational. Science has its own peculiar blinders and limitations that confront the same dilemmas of the yogi and the commissar over ends and means but in a different context.

The ideological problem of *The Call Girls* is the dominant theme of most of Koestler's writing—the search for the means of man's survival as a species in the face of an apparently insatiable compulsion to self-destruction. Here the dilemma of means is that they must reflect the values that make life meaningful in the first place. And the dilemma of ends is that they are determined in the final analysis not by scientists, but by politicians who are still laboring under the assumptions of the commissars. In the search itself, however, science plays a dual role, much like the Janus effect of holons; it is modern science that has placed in the hands of politicians the instruments of total destruction and at the same time has been called upon to save mankind.

The novel is structured around a series of dialogues that represent contending scientific approaches to the problem of survival. Each branch of science is personified in a different character who sees his own field as the answer. Because science combines with strong egos and because many of the contending solutions are mutually exclusive, science fails to offer the way out. The major problem is the lack of a master paradigm that will combine what is relevant in each and still keep in sight the goal of science—the salvation of man. Koestler believes that in his concept of holons and hierarchy, he is on the right track in the discovery of such a paradigm. But as the dilemma of the novel makes clear, a theoretical solution is still a long way from a political solution.

The view of politics that emerges from *The Call-Girls* is considerably more detached than was the case with Koestler's early writing. The commitment remains as strong as ever, but the passion is gone. There is the same combination of optimism and pessimism, but now with a touch of bemused humor. Koestler is more of a spectator to the events of this novel than was the case of his early work.

This newfound perspective as a spectator allows him to indulge in a drole humor when describing certain character types that was lacking previously. In *The Age of Longing,* he had employed occasional sarcasm that fairly dripped with venom, but in *The Call-Girls,* it is a mellow sort of humor that is not as likely to offend even the objects of its jabs. In addition, Koestler also created his first plausible feminine portraits. It is a novel that contains some of Koestler's best fictional writing and a display of his wit that is both novel and refreshingly unexpected. It is a forceful and at times compelling story of a genuine problem of the twentieth century.

1 The Intellectual "Call-Girls"

Throughout his career as a writer, Koestler has always shown a marked disdain for a certain class of intellectuals. Ordinarily they are the sophists, as in the example of *The Age of Longing,* who are allied with the new barbarians by an unwillingness to think through the logical consequences of their ideas. In his early political fiction they are the fellow travelers of the Communist party. In *The Call-Girls,* however, Koestler broadens his target considerably to include apparently intellectuals generally. Here it is not so much a question of simple sophistry, though that is certainly present, as the general prostitution of scientific theories that are not mere sophistry. It makes little difference here whether or not the individuals are on the side of angels or devils, they are both parodied by Koestler with an even-handed humor that lumps friends and foes alike into the same cauldron of impotence.

The specific intellectuals targeted in *The Call-Girls* are the elite of the scientific and intellectual world. They are Nobel Prize winners, distinguished authors and poets, popular personalities who are known even to the common man. As the cream of their class, they are nevertheless portrayed as intellectual "call-girls" who populate the international guest lecture circuit. They are present at every major conference or symposium dealing with the problem of the human condition. As a class they suffer from political impotence; their problem is an inability to wed their massive intellects and genuine scientific contributions to the ordinary cannons of political action. Their political impotence, however, is in inverse proportion to their own sense of importance. By the conclusion of the novel, the reader is uncertain whether he hopes they will succeed or fail in joining scientific theories to political acts.

The setting for the novel is one of those international conferences that has been called specifically to save the world from its follies. It is, no doubt, much like dozens of such conferences that Koestler himself has attended. The participants are among the most prestigious names in science, with a scattering of representatives from the humanities. Their very success as individuals, however, is their gravest weakness; they are unable to see the problems of science and survival except from their own perspectives. One of the wives remarks at a cocktail party on the eve of the meeting;

The call-girls are getting more moth-eaten every year. Even the younger ones look as if they had spent the night on a shelf in the public library. I wonder why they are so dull, and the more they cultivate their eccentricities, the duller. Could it be the effect of over specialization? It is unavoidable, but it may lead to a kind of stunted personality, because they feel more and more passionate about lesser and lesser fragments of the world.[1]

The conference was called by Nobel Prize winner Nikolai Solovief. He gave it the title "Approaches to Survival." The stated purpose was to bring together in one place the greatest scientific minds in the world for the single purpose of saving the world. Although Nikolai is portrayed as not especially optimistic about the chances for success, he nevertheless feels a moral compulsion to try. His model for a successful effort by scientists to change the world is the famous letter from Albert Einstein to President Roosevelt in 1939 in which the great scientist had set the stage for the development of the atom bomb. The president had accepted the letter and with it Einstein's offer to help. Solovief vaguely hopes that the symposium will draft a similar letter to the American president with similar results. The letter was his basis for optimism. It was historical proof that the scientific community could talk to the political elites and have an impact on events not several decades removed.

Nikolai had participated in the Los Altamos project that followed Einstein's letter. But when the end result of that project turned out to be Hiroshima, Nikolai suffered from a deep sense of guilt over his own role in the development of the bomb. He never recovered from it and devoted the rest of his career to the peaceful application of science. He knew first hand that the science that could save the world had also placed the world in its present danger.

In spite of the importance attributed to the conference by Nikolai and its participants, there is an aura of fantasy about it from the beginning. The reader does not really expect the scientists to solve the problem. Instead, he is treated to a *tour de force* of various scientific panaceas for the problem, none of which are likely to be politically acceptable. The very location of the conference lends itself to this make-believe atmosphere; it is located in an out-of-the-way center nestled snugly in the Swiss Alps in the pure and rarified air of a corner of Europe that the entire twentieth century seems to have passed by. Even the formal sponsor for the conference, "The Foundation for Promoting Love among Nations," sounds eccentric. The sponsor, like the participants, lives in the remote, rarified atmosphere of abstractions that can barely see into the valley below where most people live.

From the very beginning, Nikolai foresees that his major problem will be in getting the participants to agree on a single definition of the dimensions of the problem itself. In 1939, when Einstein wrote his letter, the scientific community had a common language in the study of theoretical physics, knew what the problems were, and knew what work had to be done to solve them. Now, he laments, "We cannot even define the problem. Each of us has a different definition. And that, precisely, defines our problem."[2] How can science save the world if the scientists do not know how to go about it? The impression Koestler portrays is a mixture of comedy and tragedy. There is a grim, almost gallows humor, in the efforts of these often pompous dilettantes to grapple with a practical problem of overwhelming importance. As the reader watches the spectacle unfold, the symposium comes to resemble the Mad Hatter's tea party more than the popular image of sedate and slightly stuffy scientists seriously debating world problems. The conference itself is something of a chimera, but it is about serious business nonetheless.

It is Nikolai's single-minded obsession with saving the world that gives dramatic seriousness to the conference. In his picture of Nikolai, Koestler is very much in earnest, and he sketches him without the humorous irony reserved for most of the others. Nikolai sees the meeting as a "school for Cassandras." It is a familiar symbol in Koestler's work. Shortly after publication of *The Age of Longing*, Koestler had described himself as "Cassandra gone hoarse," meaning that since no one was listening to his warnings any longer, he had nothing further to say on politics. When Nikolai again picks up this symbolism, it is with an increased awareness that in Greek mythology Cassandra was fated to be right, but that no one would recognize the truth she spoke. This is the same fate as "Approaches to Survival"; it is Koestler's way of saying that science is theoretically correct, but that no one will listen.

As the conference convenes, it is under the shadow of an impending global war. In the context of the novel, it is impossible to know whether or not this is an exaggerated reading of events reported in the newspapers or whether it is intended to be a curtainraiser for World War III. In the final analysis it may not matter. If this is not a crisis, then there will be one eventually and the same problem of survival will again confront science. Of the participants, only Nikolai seems to be capable of submerging his own ego sufficiently to see the full depths and dimensions of the crisis. But this only serves to make him a more tragic figure because, unlike the more fortunate Einstein, he has no clearly definable enemy such as the Nazis. He does not face the prospects of a war that can be won or lost by weaponry in the conventional sense of the term. Before the catastrophe can be averted, he knows that science must confront the problem morally and not merely with a clinical detachment. But morality is the oldest casualty of the scientific outlook. The babble of tongues at the meeting is itself a reflection of the problem. Science, having already destroyed the idea of a unity between the moral and the rational, is now called upon to reconstitute the two poles. But modern science has no ground upon which it can build a solution and must grope in the dark like everyone else. "Remember Archimedes: 'Give me but one firm spot in the universe to stand on and I will move the earth.' We have no firm spot to stand on. In fact, no moral leg to stand on."[3]

II *The Structure of the Arguments*

The various arguments over the best way for science to be employed in the salvation of the species are presented in the form of a series of papers delivered over the week of the conference. All the arguments have been presented before at other similar meetings and most of the participants are en route to still other conferences after this one adjourns. They have long since memorized each other's positions, and they expect few surprises. It is a highly ritualized, almost symbolic affair.

The debate between the contending ideas is a purely theoretical one. There is no distracting action outside the presentations to take away from a focus on the ideas. It is Koestler at his very best, where the heroes are ideas and not persons. The theories are presented in the abstract and counterarguments follow, but for the most part there are no demonstrably conclusive results of any position, except in the unfortunate case of the neurosurgeon. It is part of the tragedy of science in the modern world that its most hopeful and promising ideas remain abstractions. But at the same time, the reader is left with a sense of relief that many of the ideas remain in the laboratories and are not realized.

Although the names of the participants are fictitious, the scientific theories and experiments described in the novel are not. All of the papers represent actual work in contemporary science. But with the exception of Nikolai, the scientists themselves are unable to envision the moral dimensions of their work. The incongruity between scientific maturity and moral backwardness sustains the tragicomic theme of the novel.

The major scientific propositions at the symposium are divided into two fairly broad and opposing camps: the materialists and the nonmaterialists. It is the yogi-commissar dichotomy in a new format. These two main camps are in turn divided into a larger number of subspecies of argument (indeed each participant is a walking subspecies of argument in his own person). The leading representatives of these antagonistic positions are Professor Hector Burch for the materialists and Nikolai for the nonmaterialists. The former is a behaviorist who resembles B. F. Skinner very closely. Nikolai, on the other hand, is a humanistically inclined physicist whose philosophy of science seems to be a carbon copy of Koestler's. The other participants at the symposium group themselves around these two leading figures at various distances. But whatever the distance, they remain opposite poles of thought, and like the yogi and the commissar, there is no evident middle ground between them. In the end a choice must be made between materialism or nonmaterialism.

A distinguishing feature of this dichotomy in *The Call-Girls* is its similarity to the yogi-commissar continuum as well as its differences from that earlier model. First of all, it should be noted that materialism versus nonmaterialism is not conceived as ends versus means. The materialism of Burch, for example, is the same as the commissar's and is concerned with ends and not means. But by the same token, Nikolai's nonmaterialist science is ends-oriented too. Neither has very much in common with the yogi ethic of means. Insofar as Burch and Nikolai represent opposite ends of the scientific spectrum, neither leaves any room for a political ethic of pure means. Whatever may be said of Burch's affinity with the commissar, Nikolai is neither yogi nor commissar as Koestler first used those terms. While the commissar mentality remains in the person of Burch, there is no more yogi.

Burch is the quintessence of everything Koestler despises in modern science. In addition to his materialism, he is dogmatic and narrow-minded and refuses to believe in anything outside of his own laboratory: "Show me a slice of your super-ego under the microscope," he says, "and I will believe in its existence."[4] He can develop a science of the brain, because he can see it, but not a science of the mind, because "mind" suggests something nonmaterial. To postulate even the existence of the mind as distinct from the brain is an act of superstition. He has what Koestler contemptuously refers to as a "ratomorphic" view of mankind—that is, he refuses to believe that man as a species has any characteristics that are not also observable in a laboratory rat. What can be done by and to rats in an experiment can just as easily be repeated in politics. It is all a question of reducing behavior to its most elementary components: "I am concerned with the experimental study of the conditioning of lower mammals and the application of these techniques to our educational system. That is social engineering, based on hard facts, not nebulous speculation."[5]

Burch delivers his paper on the first day of the symposium and thus sets the tone for the debates that follow. He is the adversary of the nonmaterialists. Basically he argues that the differences between rats and men are quantitative and not qualitative. Men's values, he says, are no more than conditioned reflexes that are in response to their social environment. The solution to the problem of human aggression is thus comparatively simple—change the environment, and the responses by men to their environment will automatically change. It is basically the same argument as the commissar's for change from without. Burch contends that scientists already know how to describe, predict, and hence control human behavior. The relationship between theory and practice is already fully understood, and all that remains to be done is to apply those theories on a mass scale. Indeed, he argues that experiments have already begun on a limited scale, and it is only a matter of time before they are applied on a mass level.[6] The future survival of the human race depends, he solemnly declares, upon the willingness of governments to follow the behaviorist trail blazed by B. F. Skinner.

Nikolai, on the other hand, has a different perspective altogether. His view is a product of his occult ideas about the origins of scientific creativity, considered eccentric or "romantic" by most of his colleagues. His career in theoretical physics was an offshoot of music. He had been a musical prodigy as a child. His interest in mathematics was awakened through an accidental reading of Pythagoras, who had first discovered that musical scales could be expressed in mathematical terms. Later he found that the Pythagorian fantasy had been rediscovered by Johannes Kepler who then used its mysticism to build the foundations of modern astronomy. To the young Nikolai, this discovery meant that the universe spoke in rational terms and that the basis for rationality was mathematics. He was determined to find the key to universal understanding: "He now believed, with almost religious fervor, that the mystery of the universe was contained in the equations which governed the ballet of the tiny particles inside the atom, and in the Wagnerian grand opera, performed by comets, stars, and galaxies."[7]

In later years, especially after Hiroshima, Nikolai lost much of his youthful enthusiasm. The earlier harmony of music and physics broke down with the erratic behavior of subatomic particles. The world of the modern physicist had become a "mad wonderland" where an electron could be in two places at once or no place at all. Quoting Nils Bohr, his motto of modern science was "the madder the better."[8] The materialist universe of Burch had collapsed, but there was as yet nothing to take its place as an organizing principle. His own work in physics that had won for him the Nobel Prize he saw as irrational in the language of all prior science, and he christened his discoveries with a name borrowed from Eastern mysticism combined with Western science. Modern science, he believed, could only be approached as a blend of the occult and the rational.

By placing Nikolai and Burch at separate poles, Koestler is making several points. First, it is a reaffirmation of his long-standing belief that both the occult and the rational are aspects of human nature. Here Nikolai symbolizes the ideal type for the latter half of the twentieth century—the new man to replace the image of the commissar. But Nikolai pays a price for combining these two poles in his character. Reason is torn between a poetic and a purely rational mode of expression. The tension between poetic reason and scientific reason is intensified in *The Call-Girls* moreso than in any other novel by Koestler. Burch still clings to the notion that science has progressed from superstition and religion to the final triumph of scientific materialism. Nikolai knows better, but he cannot quite articulate this insight in the commonly accepted language of scientific discourse.

In a limited sense, Nikolai and Burch are at opposite ends of a continuum that looks much like that of the yogi and the commissar. The major difference in *The Call-Girls* is that the distance between the poles has considerably narrowed. Nikolai is haunted by the fear that Burch máy be right, just as Rubashov was fearful that No. 1 might be in the right.[9] He finds difficulty stating his vision of a higher than material reality. When Nikolai is asked at one point, "What is serious?", he replies, enigmatically, "A toothache is serious."[10] It is an echo of Rubashov's grammatical fiction where a toothache is symbolic of his moral consciousness.

III   *The Approaches to Survival*

The one thing the participants of the symposium all seem to have in common is a shared belief that their own branch of science has a solution to the problem. The only limited exceptions to this are the poet Sir Evelyn Blood, and a priest, Tony Caspari, neither of whom stands within the scientific community as understood and defined by the others. There is a measure of intended irony in the presumption of the call-girls to have an answer to something when they are not collectively certain of the question. None of them doubts that science will save the day if given a chance, but there is no consensus as to the proper scope and nature of science. They are unable to agree on the root causes of the problem itself, much less on any solution that would logically follow from such agreement. They are "worse than politicians," one of them remarks, because while most politicians are ham actors to begin with, the academic types suffer from an arrested emotional development:

And what is their truth? . . . It seems . . . that each of them possesses a small fragment of the Truth which he believes to be the Whole Truth, which he carries around in his pocket like tarnished bubblegum, and blows it up on solemn occasions to prove that it contains the ultimate mystery of the universe. Discussion? Interdisciplinary dialogue? There is no such thing, except in the printed program. When the dialogue is supposed to start, each gets his own bubble-gum out and blows it into the others' faces.[11]

The presentation of these "bubble-gum" arguments forms the basic structure of the call-girl arguments. Appropriately, it is Burch who makes the first such presentation: "All that the technology of behavior needed to solve the problems of mankind were scientifically control-led schedules of positive and negative reinforcements. To talk about good or bad, freedom, dignity and purpose was antiquated poppy-cock."[12]

In his general conception, thought not in all of its details, Burch is supported by a number of others. Chief among them is Doctor Otto von Halder, who is impressed with behaviorism but adds a few twists of his own. Halder is an anthropologist who has been working with animals in order to understand the root causes of human aggression. His work has convinced him that man is primarily a killer-animal, a species of assassins. Man, at present, is engaged in something that resembles a Hobbesian state of nature, a war of all against all: "If we deny it, if we do not dare to face the facts about our own nature, then there is no hope for the remedy."[13] His own remedy for aggression is to ritualize it, to channel the killer instinct into symbolic displays, such as gladiator events. He apparently believes that the gladiators themselves will willingly accept their assigned role as surrogates for popular passions. Koestler's first novel, *The Gladiators*, may rightly be taken as Koestler's answer to Halder on this proposal.

Halder, however, is not content to merely generalize about his plan; he also suggests specific examples of this psychology. The best example, he duly notes, is to be found in the "Hate Weeks" of George Orwell's *Nineteen Eighty-Four*. Orwell had obviously regarded this ritual as damnable, but Halder suggests there is another way to look at it. "Here you have the classic abreaction therapy on a mass scale," he says.[14] The problem with Orwell's interpretation was that he had misunderstood the social function of Hate Week. Under more con-trolled circumstances, such an exercise could have the beneficial effect of allowing pent-up emotions to be released in less harmful ways.

Nikolai, of course, was swift in his rebuttal of Halder. He and several others noted that Halder had been a Nazi during World War II and thus the ritualization of Hate Week was perhaps a natural turn of his mind. What Nikolai does by this association is to establish a link between behavioral psychology and totalitarian political movements. The materialism of Halder is like the materialism of the commissar, with equally predictable political consequences.

In partial agreement with Burch and Halder is Doctor Horace Wyndham, an internationally famous specialist on infant behavior. His own research suggests that the problem of learning aggressive behavior begins with childbirth. Modern methods of delivery psychologically scar children for life. Improved methods of delivery, combined with the proper toilet training, will have the effect of vastly increasing the IQs of babies, who will in turn solve the problem of aggression—smarter babies will be less aggressive. These improved techniques can be aided by chemically induced alterations in the fetus that will significantly alter brain capacity prior to birth.[15]

But the behaviorists are skeptical. Even assuming the truth of Wyndham's controversial experiments, the result will simply be a species of killers with superior intellect, and all the more dangerous because of it. The proposed solution would only make sense if one accepted what Halder considers the dubious proposition that the cause of aggression is a lack of intelligence. Here Halder speaks for the behaviorists and antibehaviorists as well.

Another zoologist who has been working with animals in the study of human aggression, Doctor Harriet Epsom, has an entirely different series of conclusions that either Halder or Wyndham. Her reaction to the notion that man is a killer-animal is an acidly muttered "Rot" whenever Halder makes his point. Her own work with monkeys in Africa has convinced her that aggressive behavior is "a reaction provoked by stress when it exceeds a certain limit."[16] Some examples may be increased population pressures on limited space and the like. Wars are not fought because of individual aggression, she says, but because of impersonal causes—patriotism, ethnic or tribal loyalties, etc. Soldiers fight because they are loyal to certain abstractions, not because they hate: "The individual is not a killer; the group is; and by identifying with it, the individual becomes one."[17]

The real enemy in Dr. Epsom's world is idealism. Wars are fought for words and "the worst of madmen is a saint run wild."[18] Her solution to the dilemma of the human condition is to develop a chemical that can be placed into the tapwater of everyone that will make them immune to the siren calls of politicians, churches, nations, and so forth. Furthermore, she argues, there is no logical basis for either individual or group idealism. Men's ideas about justice and ethnic identities are entirely dependent upon the accident of birth. Language, in all its forms, is the means by which the problem is expressed and any genuine solution must be one that takes into account the corrupting influence of linguistic abstractions. Language is not just that of Orwell's "newspeak," but all language at all times.

In substantial agreement with Dr. Epsom is Cesare Valenti, a world famous neurosurgeon. But he sees a link between her and Burch and his own research. His solution is for a form of neuroengineering—the placement of small electrodes in the area of the brain that is responsible for aggression which can then be controlled remotely in such a way as to completely alter behavior. This can now be done surgically and is no longer a matter of theoretical speculation but an established fact. When someone calls this a "horrible solution," Valenti reminds the audience, "We are a horrible race, living in horrible times. Perhaps we should have the courage to think of horrible remedies."[19] And to demonstrate that he is not above such coldblooded remedies, he has brought to the symposium a young lady who is the subject of such experiments. Her behavior at the remote control command of Valenti is suggestive of the fruits of neuroengineering.

Doctor Valenti's patient is presented to the audience at the conclusion of his paper. It is the dramatic high point of the conference, and everyone is enthralled as he proceeds to demonstrate the possibilities of neuroengineering. He began his experiment by reminding everyone of the theme of the conference—that all mankind would be doomed unless some solution to the problem of aggression and war could be found. Regardless of "why" man was an aggressive animal, he said, it was commonly agreed that under certain circumstances man is his own worst enemy. But now, thanks to science, man has at his disposal the means to become instead his own best friend. Experiments have conclusively proven that animal behavior can be completely controlled by the implantation of these electrodes in the brain. What this suggests to Valenti is that the brain is the center of the problem and can be controlled by simple surgery. His patient, Miss Carey, is living proof of the success and validity of his work.

It seems that Miss Carey had a case history of violent, unprovoked attacks on members of her own family. Ordinary psychoanalysis, such as that advocated by Burch, had failed to solve her problem. Finally,

as a last resort, Valenti had been called into the case because of his
expertise in neurosurgery. It was, to him at least, an experiment in
the application of theory to practice. The tiny electrodes had worked
their cure. He controlled her behavior through a remote control
device which he wore on his wrist as inconspicuously by as a watch.
By a simple turn of the dial, he could inflict either unbearable pain or
the most intense pleasures. As a result, Miss Carey looked upon
Valenti as her savior.

Unfortunately, in the midst of the demonstration, the experiment
developed problems of its own. For some unexplicable reason—
perhaps for no "reason" at all—Miss Carey suddenly developed a case
of uncontrolled hysteria as Valenti's electrodes failed to function
properly. She grabbed a knitting needle and stabbed Solovief's wife
in the arm. After a brief struggle, Valenti managed to subdue her with
a sedative, but the "bugs" in the system were painfully obvious to all.
Clearly, it would seem, neuroengineering was not yet perfected.

At the end of the novel, Miss Carey goes berserk again and sets fire
to the conference building. Fortunately the only thing destroyed are
the tape recordings of the papers presented and the subsequent
discussions. Though it prevents the public from having a record of the
symposium, it is doubtful that enlightened opinion has suffered an
irreversable loss. By the time of the fire, most of the participants are
already on their way to other conferences to deliver the same papers
all over again. Miss Carey's gesture is insanely futile, but perhaps no
more so than the symposium itself. By the time the tapes are
destroyed, the reader may harbor a secret desire that much the same
fate awaits the other conferences.

IV *Tentative Solutions*

Given the theoretical confusion and the political obstacles to be
overcome, neither Koestler or the reader seriously expect any solutions to emerge from the symposium. Nevertheless, Koestler does
put forward certain suggestions as to the direction he believes science
should move on the problem. For the most part, these suggestions
are shorthand versions of arguments that appeared earlier in *The
Ghost in the Machine* and other miscellaneous essays of the period. In
some respects, these proposals seem every bit as fantastic as those he
rejected. What distinguishes them is not their scientific qualities
alone, but rather, Koestler's ability to unite them with what he
preceives to be the twin poles of human existence: reason and
mysticism.

In addition to Nikolai, the chief spokesman for Koestler's view is, curiously, Tony Caspari, a Copertinian Brother in the Catholic Church. He seems to represent that other strand of Western thought that so fascinates Koestler, that stands outside the mainstream of modern science—the mystic. The choice by Koestler of a religious figure to convey the element of mysticism in modern science is consistent with his analysis of the mysterious origins of creativity. Caspari is not a rationalist as the other scientists understand the term, but neither is he irrational in the larger sense of the term "science" as Koestler has developed it. As Koestler had acknowledged in *The Yogi and the Commissar*, the basic framework for his understanding of science proper had come from his reading of the Christian notion of hierarchy. Hence Tony's paper, the last one to be presented, may be seen as a symbolic reunion of the mystic and the rationalist tradition that had been split during the Renaissance.

Of all the persons at the symposium, Tony is perhaps the only one who could reasonably be called a "whole person." He is gentle, modest, and unassuming. With the exception of Nikolai, he is the only one present who can lay claim to being a scientist and yet have a sense of the limitations of science too narrowly conceived. Indeed, he is the only one of the participants for whom the perjorative label "call-girl" seems inappropriate. Along with Nikolai, Tony is the only leading figure in the novel who is not satarized or parodied by Koestler. In the context of the novel, it is perhaps the highest tribute Koestler can pay to him.

What Tony argues for in his presentation is the scientifically heretical notion of mind over matter. If matter no longer exists for physicists in the nineteenth century conception, it would seem to be a logical presentation to offer a counter theory. To the most extreme materialists, such as Burch and Halder, there is no such thing as "mind." But, on the other hand, to Nikolai there is no such thing as "matter." To make his case, Tony draws upon experiments that scarcely seem to be "scientific" at first glance.

To begin with, Tony is not a member of the typical sort of Catholic Order. It is a relatively obscure one founded by an equally obscure seventeenth century saint who performed extraordinary feats of levitation "at about the same time Isaac Newton proclaimed the law of universal gravity."[20] In other words, at the same time that Newton was rationalizing certain physical laws, someone else was mystifying them. Thus the twin poles of human experience are both sundered and joined by this particular Order. Over the years the Order has experimented with their founder's feats. Some of the brothers amuse themselves with little tricks of mind over matter in games involving mathematics and the like. These experiments have been repeated and confirmed by probability theorists. "It is merely a first step," Tony says, "But it shows that the mind can perhaps one day gain complete control of the machine which is the body.[21] What Tony offers is a theory of extra sensory perception and research in human brain waves.

Despite the skepticism of most of the other members of the symposium, Tony is the only one among them who seems to offer any synthesis between the materialists and the nonmaterialists. When one of them asks him what this presentation has to do with the theme of the conference, Tony is forced to give a poetical answer. Who knows where the science of the mind will lead? What we are searching for, he says, are "The sources of the Nile." By this he means that the science of the mind, in all its aspects, has become the most important scientific problem for the modern world. It is in a knowledge of the mind that any solution to the problem confronting the symposium will have to be found.

Much to the embarassment of the others, who have listened to Tony incredulously, Nikolai defends the paper on extrasensory perception and mind over matter. The fact that the experiments with ESP seem to contradict the "so-called" laws of nature implicit in modern science does not bother him. "Relativity and Quantum theory did the same—they contradicted the laws of Nature as Newton understood them."[22] The only other participant who finds any comfort in Tony and Nikolai's views is, significantly, not a scientist but a poet, Sir Evelyn Blood. In his nonscientific defense of Tony, the reader can hear ths poetic side of Koestler speaking out against materialism: "The most monumental superstition of our century is the type of science that treats man as a salivating Pavlov dog, or an overgrown Skinner rat, or a Cricket-robot programmed by its genetic code. . . .[Such] science is a methodical form of paranoia."[23]

But the practical criticism of Tony remains. Even accepting the truth of his claims, how will such knowledge lead to a solution of the problem of survival? In answer, Tony can only fall back on a vague faith in the ultimate rationality of the universe. "By groping toward the light we are made to realize how deep the darkness around us."[24] What he aims at is a cognition of reality that transcends the world of sensory perception. It is Koestler's third level of scientific comprehension. He is uncertain of where research into ESP will lead, but he believes that through its insights mankind may be on the brink of a new Copernican revolution in science. "It may not change the world, but it may change our outlook on the world."[25]

Nikolai's attraction to Tony's paper is due in part to his guiding principle in the study of modern physics—"The madder the better." He does not share Tony's faith, but he does believe that faith springs from a mysticism about nature that he does share: "Our main trouble is that we no longer have a coherent world-view—neither the theologian nor the physicist. God is dead, but materialism is also dead, since matter has become a meaningless word. Causality, determinism, the clockwork universe of Newton have been buried without ceremony."[26]

V   *The Failure of the Conference*

Tony's paper and Nikolai's reception of it proved to be the scandal of the symposium. Even Nikolai's closest friends found it embarrassing. In turn, their reaction was a source of profound sadness for Nikolai. It meant there would be no scientific synthesis between divergent views, no dramatic telegram that would change the course of history. Recalling a passage from Shakespeare, he sadly observed, "The fault, dear Brutus, is not in our stars, but in the limits of our imagination."[27]

When Nikolai sets out to summarize the results of the conference for the others in closing, it is with an overwhelming sense of pessimism. Nature, he says, in the form of its evolutionary process, has let men down in the development of his mind. Man must, as a result, now assume full and complete responsibility for the direction of his future evolution: "If we presume to call ourselves men of science, we must work up the courage to propose the radical remedies which might give humanity a chance of survival. We cannot wait for another hundred thousand years, hoping for a favorable mutation to remedy our ills. We must engineer that mutation ourselves, by biological methods that are within our reach—or soon will be."[28]

The spectacle of aggression is endemic in the mind of the species, he asserts. A recognition of it "was our point of departure." The science of the mind is the first step in coming to grips with the problem of survival. Here one can see the crucial role Koestler's trilogy on the science of the mind occupies in terms of his prior political writing. It points to the unity of his fictional and scientific writing. The dilemma of the two periods is also in evidence—the inability to translate theory into practice.

As the conference breaks up and the call-girls are already on their way to other meetings, Koestler once more reminds the reader of the precariousness of modern times. "In view of the international situation, however, nobody could be sure whether they would reach their destination."[29] It is then that Nikolai recalls from the Book of Genesis, God had created the world from chaos in six days—the same length of time as the symposium "Approaches to Survival." It was also about the same length of time that it would take man to undo Creation and substitute a new form of chaos by simply pushing a few buttons. Rhetorically, Koestler asks the reader if the final world war has already sounded—there are sirens down in the town in the valley. And then he has Nikolai answer with a shrug: "He could not care less." But in spite of appearances on the outside, Nikolai does care. As the last participant to depart the conference center, Harriet Epsom observes of him, "He looks like the captain of a sinking ship, determined to go down with it."[30]

CHAPTER 9

A Crusader Without A Cross

IN spite of its diversity, there is a unity to Koestler's work that emcompasses both the fictional and nonfictional portions. That unity may be found in Koestler's search for a rational structure of reason that can be translated from theory into practice in the human condition. That search for a modern praxis is essentially a political quest as opposed, for example, to a religious one. But at the same time, his, commitment to the unity of theory and practice in politics takes on much of the form of a religious passion: "a crusade without a cross, a fervent belief without faith," as Manes Sperber has put it.[1]

The unity of theory and practice is not merely an abstract problem for Koestler. It is preeminently a practical one, and that is the source of its political base. The problem is all the more pressing in the contemporary world, he argues, because the preponderence of intellectual weight is against his own notion that a materialistic conception of reason in the Newtonian mold is the root of the modern political dilemma. His great protagonist is the prevasive argument of modernity that truth is in the mind and not in the external world. His fear, however, is that his critics may be right. In an echo of Koestler's concern, George Orwell stated the problem most succinctly in *Nineteen Eighty-Four:* "And what was terrifying was not that they would kill you for thinking otherwise, but that they might be right. For, after all, how do we know that two and two makes four? Or that the law of gravity works? Or that the past is unchangeable? If the past and the external world exist only in the mind, and if the mind itself is controllable—what then."[2]

In *Darkness at Noon,* Rubashov had faced an identical question: What if No. 1 was in the right, and Gletkin is the new man of the future—what then? Or again, in *The Call-Girls,* Nikolai found himself face to face with the same question posed by the behaviorists: What if they are right—what then? Rubashov tacitly agreed with

Gletkin when he consented to the confession—it was ideologically the "correct" response and helped establish the party rule that truth was in the mind, that is to say, "ideological." Nikolai, on the other hand, made no such concession, but his response was hardly satisfactory to the others at the symposium. But whatever his fictional characters may do, Koestler has never accepted that modern argument. Instead there is a tension between his rejection of it and a fear that it may after all be right. This tension is the wellspring of his own creativity and the consternation of so many of his critics.

In some respects Koestler is less of a professional writer than a witness to his time. He is capable of exceptionally fine writing style and dramatic intensity, as in *Darkness at Noon,* for example. But he never gives the impression of having polished his style much beyond the bare mechanics necessary to get his points across to his readers. In a lesser author, this would be a major drawback that could destroy a career. That this has never happened to Koestler, in spite of some rather poorly received novels from time to time, may be attributed largely to the power of his message, which has managed to transcend the style of its presentation. His ideas are so powerfully stated that there have been surprisingly few criticisms of style alone.[3] Because of this, most critics have, rightly, been more interested in his message then the form by which it has been presented.

In general, Koestler's critics may be divided into two categories: those who believe that the modern unity of theory and practice as materialistic reason is a mistake, and those who do not. The former have tended to side with Koestler and the latter against him. This pattern has held true for his fiction as well as for his nonfiction. Thus the fundamental thematic unity of his work is mirrored by an opposing unity among those critics who have accepted the basic structure of the modernist arguments. Many of the same grounds Maurice Merleau-Ponty found for criticizing *Darkness at Noon,* for example, are echoed by the most critical reviews of Koestler's trilogy on the science of the mind.

It will be useful, therefore, if Koestler's critics are divided into the two basic categories that conform to the division of his work into its fictional and nonfictional aspects. At the same time, the similarity of criticisms of both phases should be noted. What unites such seemingly disparate critics as Communists, fellow travelers, academics, and apolitical scientists is their often common assumption that Koestler is engaged in an assault on reason itself. There is frequently an inability to take seriously the tension in his writing between the

poles. All too often, this tension has appeared to be simply contradic-
tionory or inconsistant. In a sense there is some justification to point
out these inconsistancies and contradictions. But what writer who has
tried to reconcile these extremes has not been inconsistant? It is
insufficient to simply note these surface irregularities unless the
deeper strength and unity is also pointed out. An appreciation of the
unity does not resolve the tensions, but it does make them more
understandable.

I   *Communism and* Darkness at Noon

Darkness at Noon is the centerpiece of Koestler's exploration of the
dilemma of ends and means. The problem is there with or without the
addition of the modern revolutionary ethos, but it is intensified by the
revolutionary personality. In the revolutionary context, the dilemma
is intensified far beyond that of times past. Hence it is not surprising
that the most systematic criticisms of Koestler's political world view
should concentrate on this particular novel. By considering those
criticisms in some detail here, it is possible to obtain a better picture
of the thrust of Koestler's own arguments. His position is, in part,
defined by the nature of the opposition.

The most important and systematic attacks on Koestler in general
and on *Darkness at Noon* in particular came from France in the
aftermath of World War II. The novel was originally published after
the outbreak of the war and after the fall of France in 1940. Because of
this, the novel did not have a major critical audience outside of the
English-speaking world until after 1945. When the novel was translated into French as *Le Zéro et l'Infini* in 1946, it immediately became
a *cause cèlèbre* and a serious political issue among French Communists and their fellow travelers.

The initial reaction of French Communists was to destroy whatever
copies they could in hopes that they could prevent its dissemination.
When that failed, a two-pronged counterattack was launched by the
party on the one hand and by influential fellow travelers led by Jean
Paul Sartre and Maurice Merleau-Ponty on the other. The pages of
Sartre's *Les Temps Modernes* were in the forefront of the attack. The
novel was especially crucial in 1946 because that coincided with the
first referendum in France since before the war, and the Communists
stood to gain or lose according to their strength at the voting polls.[4]
The issue of Stalin and the French Communist party figured promi-
nately in electoral politics that year. In his autobiography, Koestler
attributed a major reason for the defeat of the Communists at the polls

that year to the controversy that surrounded his book. [5] The validity of his claim is difficult to measure. Some contemporary French newspapers have tended to discount the claim, since it assumes a great deal about ideological influences on voting behavior, which are always controversial and difficult to assess. But there can be no doubt of the importance attributed to the novel by the French Left. [6]

Roger Garaudy wrote what may be termed the "orthodox" party response that was simultaneously critical of *Les Temps Modernes* and Sartre on one side and *Le Zéro et l'Infini* on the other. In his *Literature of the Graveyard*, he described the novel as "that detective story with a metaphysical plot." [7] The problem with Koestler's thesis, he wrote, was that the dilemma of ends and means was "abstract"— that is, false. Rubashov could not be considered as a true revolutionary type because no Marxist would accept the notion that there was indeed a problem of ends and means. Lenin's concept of the dictatorship of the proletariat had long since resolved that question. To accept Koestler's presentation of revolution "robs us of the virile and positive joy of adherence and creation" to be found in Stalin's forging of a Communist state. [8]

Years later, when Garaudy himself was expelled from the French Communist party, he wrote that he saw no reason to alter his first assessment of Koestler as an antirevolutionary writer. [9] For Garaudy and the orthodox party members, the problems posed by Koestler could be favorably resolved by a simple reduction of the question to its dialectical opposite; the problem of the confessions would disappear, if only Koestler and his readers would assume the guilt of Rubashov instead of his innocence. [10] The novel, Garaudy said, posed only metaphysical problems characteristic of bourgeois liberalism and need be treated as nothing more than a propaganda tract against Stalin. The obsequious court Garaudy paid to the party line is probably more revealing of the sterility of thought in the French Communist party than as a commentary on Koestler.

An entirely different order of criticism, however, is to be found in the imaginative and complex rebuttal to *Le Zéro et l'Infini* by Maurice Merleau-Ponty. He was able to advance a more telling criticism than Garaudy for two closely related reasons. First, his already established reputation as one of the major French authors of the century insured a greater insightfulness and mastery of argument than Garaudy could ever hope to muster. Secondly, Merleau-Ponty was never a member of the Communisty party, but always remained a fellow traveler. Despite a great deal of party invective directed against him and

Sartre, during the 1940s in particular he was one of its most ardent supporters and apologists for Stalin. This degree of orthodox independence left him with greater flexability and originality in forming a response than Garaudy.

His critique of Koestler was published as *Humanism and Terror* in 1947 and was taken largely from essays that had appeared earlier in the pages of *Les Temps Modernes*. As a defense of revolutionary terror, it is, in its own right, an essay that ranks among the major revolutionary tracts of the twentieth century. The logic and thesis of the essay is essentially the same as that suggested nearly a quarter of a century earlier by Trotsky in *The Defense of Terrorism*.[11] The argument is that of Gletkin, that the end will justify the means and that the party is the historically chosen vehicle to reach those ends. To his own satisfaction, Merleau-Ponty believed that he had completely refuted Koestler through a series of complex dialectical arguments that proved the superiority of Stalin's Russia over every other system of government.

The beginning point of Merleau-Ponty's dialectic against Koestler was the notion that questions of political rights and wrongs could never be separated from the true nature of the political regime under discussion. All crimes, he said, are political in nature and are not factual in any objective sense as Koestler has implied. Because the regime that alone stood for the progressive forces in history was headed by Stalin in the 1930s, all crimes supposedly committed under his rule could only be judged from the Stalinist perspective. The only valid criticism of Gletkin, for example, would be one that turned on the question of whether or not his actions advanced or retarded the future society the party was creating in Russia. "The present and the future," he wrote, "are not the object of science but of *construction* and *action*."[12] It was a candid admission that the revolutionary praxis was not built on science, as Koestler saw, but on a will to power in the sense of Nietzsche. He argued that the actions of Stalin during the Purge Trials were justified because they were based on the moral principles of the future classless society and not the decadant morals of the bourgeois past; "a revolution does not define crimes according to the established law but in accordance with the law of the society it wishes to create."[13]

The fatal flaw of *Le Zero et l'Infini*, he went on to say, was in its failure to make clear the distinction all Marxists make between "subjective" and "objective" consciousness. The former belongs to the past and the latter is the vision of the future, associated with

Rubashov and Gletkin respectively. "Gletkin stands for humanity conscious of its own material roots; he is the realization of what Rubashov has always spoken. . . . Once humanism [Gletkin] attempts to fulfill itself with any consistancy, it becomes transformed into its opposite, namely, violence."[14]

In *Humanism and Terror,* Gletkin is portrayed as the representative of insitutional humanism under Stalin and hence the embodiment of an objective political consciousness. He appears as inhuman only because he is not judged from the perspective of the perfected consciousness of the future. Furthermore, he is condemned to deal with such atavistic creatures as Rubashov who know nothing of the future. Hence it is that his profound love for mankind manifests itself to the outsider who does not share this revolutionary consciousness, such as Koestler, as an irrational terror. The outsider does not grasp the dialectics of revolutionary praxis. The Purge Trials can only be understood by those who know they are constructing the future and not attempting vainly to preserve the past. Only the genuine revolutionary can comprehend the reality of the present within its dialectical context—as the future about to be born.[15] "The Trials remain on a subjective level . . . because they bear upon facts still open toward the future, which consequently are not yet univocal and are only definitively criminal in character when they are viewed from the perspective of the future held by men in power."[16]

Because Koestler writes from the perspective of the past and present only, Merleau-Ponty argues, his is a subjective view of the trials. Koestler cannot sit in judgement of the trials because he cannot see the problem dialectically; there is no synthesis to Koestler's dilemma of ends and means, but only opposites that are ultimately irreconcilable. The rationality of the trials is not in the past or present but in the future society Stalin was in the process of building. That future will be rational, he wrote, "because it is the extrapolation and conclusion of the logic of the present."[17] To fully understand the trials it is necessary to keep in mind the logic of the dictatorship of the proletariat: "The dictatorship of the truth will always be the dictatorship of a group, and to those who do not share it, it will appear purely arbitrary. A revolution, even when founded on a philosophy of history, is a forced revolution and it is violence; correlatively, opposition in the name of humanism, can be counterrevolutionary."[18]

Koestler's problem of ends and means, says Merleau-Ponty, is a bourgeois problem and not a Marxist one. The source of Stalin's terror is not to be found in Stalin or Gletkin, but rather in the refusal of the anti-Stalinist elements to accept him and the party as the embodiment of the dictatorship of the proletariat: "either one wants to make a revolution, in which case one has to handle what it involves, or else seek at every moment to treat every man as an end in himself."[19] It is Koestler's failing, as distinguished from the true humanist, that he is concerned with men as ends in themselves and not as means alone.

At the practical level, Merleau-Ponty's criticism of Koestler is accurate—he did balk at theories of politics that treat men as means to some other end. But the point is not quite so unambiguous as Merleau-Ponty suggests. There is a distinction between the theoretical level of argument and the practical level in Koestler. On the theoretical level, when the bottom line had been reached, he was prepared to say that the end would justify the means, at least on a small scale and when the end results were reasonably predictable. But at the practical level of political action, Koestler tended to instinctively side against the commissar argument. What Merleau-Ponty failed to notice was the ambiguity and tension in Koestler as the reader moves back and forth between the purely theoretical level and the practical one.

A final point also needs to be made with regard to the nature of Merleau-Ponty's criticism of Koestler. For a number of years it has been fashionable to suggest that those fellow travelers and intellectuals who supported Communism in the 1930s and 1940s are an example of political neophytes duped by the Machiavellianism of a cynical party. This thesis argues that, for most, when they discovered the error of their ways in the wake of the Moscow Purge Trials, they changed to become foes of Communism in the 1940s and 1950s. As an interpretation of the intellectual history of the period, such a thesis is only partly true. Arthur Koestler and other contributors to the very influential *The God That Failed* in 1949 helped to foster this impression. But it is only one aspect of the history of the period. The other, and in many ways far more absorbing, story is composed of those intellectuals of the caliber of Merleau-Ponty who knew exactly what they were doing in a defense of Stalin and were quite willing to make their case public.[20]

II *The Purge Trials and Academic Critics*

The academic and scholarly critiques of Koestler's ideas on revolution have taken a considerably different tack than did Merleau-Ponty. Here the issues have often been narrower in focus, but they contain implications that go beyond surface criticism. On the surface, they have tended to be critiques of *Darkness at Noon* as a factual portrait of the Purge Trials. There is a frequent denial that anyone ever confessed as a "last service to the Party." At a deeper level, however, they raise the issue of the relationship of political theory to the practice of politics, at least among elites. The question involves the relationship between theoretical Marxism and the Moscow Purge Trials—Is there any link between them? While the basic question does not admit of any final, definitive answer, it lies at the heart of much academic criticism of *Darkness at Noon.*

If Koestler had chosen to argue that *Darkness at Noon* was basically a symbolic argument, he could have claimed a certain poetic license in the creation of fictional characters and incidents. But neither he nor any of his commentators have ever seen the events described as purely fictional in the conventional sense of the term—that is, as constructed out of whole cloth. Koestler has always claimed, and his critics have agreed, that the events were meant to be realistic portrayals of real events. Furthermore, since Koestler's real heroes have always been ideas rather than persons as such, the tendency to see his novels as a fictional cover for political commentary at a high level of generalization is not misplaced.

The most common counterargument on the role of ideology in the Purge Trials is the thesis that such a phenomenon is the end result of tyrannical government based on coercion and not a revolutionary logic. It denies that there is any ideological component in the psyche of the victims that would lead them to identify themselves with their accusors in the party or with the perverted ends of the original revolution. The explanation of the Purge Trials, therefore, is to be found in the megalomania of Stalin. Issac Deutscher, in his influential biographies of Stalin and Trotsky, for example, argued that the confessions were a result of pure torture and had nothing to do with any logical terror in Marxism.[21] For others, the trials seemed in retrospect to take on a vaguely Kafkaesque quality that in turn makes the confessions incomprehensible to the accusor, accused, and outside world as well.[22] Adam Ulam, in *The New Face of Soviet Totalitariansim,* rejected the ideological argument altogether:

The truth is simpler and more vulgar. . . . For it is clear that we see here not cruelty and inhumanity at the service of a great social or political mission, no Dostoyevskian Grand Inquisitor sacrificing the happiness of human beings for his dreams of historical purpose of mankind, but simply violent and nasty criminality, the products of sadism, envy, and fear, and the results of unbridled power. The imaginative efforts of Koestler . . . stand revealed as wide of the mark. [23]

The notion that the victims involuntarily confessed as a result of torture has been reinforced by Robert Tucker and Stephen Cohen in their translation of the verbatum record of the 1938 trials. In reviewing the testimony of Bukharin at those trials, they explicitly rejected Koestler's arguments. Tucker's introductory statement, "Burkharin agreed to participate in the trial only under some kind of duress," carries with it a great deal of scholarly authority. [24] Cohen's separate study on Bukharin, which is undoubtably the most thorough work to date, also agrees with Tucker's analysis of the transcript. [25] Thus the problem seems to be shifted back onto Koestler to defend his thesis.

In defense of Koestler's thesis, several things should be pointed out. First of all, Koestler never said that Bukharin, or anyone else in particular, was the model for Rubashov. In the frontpiece to *Darkness at Noon,* Koestler described Rubashov as a "synthesis of a number of men" whom he personally knew were victims of the purges. Furthermore, it is a serious misreading of *Darkness at Noon* to allege that Koestler offered Rubashov's story as *the* explanation for the trials. He says, on the contrary, quite the opposite: "Some were silenced by physical fear . . . some hoped to save their heads; others at least to save their wives or sons from the clutches of the Gletkins. *The best of them* kept silent in order to do a last service to the party" (italics added). [26]

It is important to note that in Koestler's thesis on the nature of the confessions as a "last service to the party" he focused only on what he called "the best of them"—that is, the most ideologically motivated. The same point can be made with regard to the role of ideas in his other novels. That is to say that Koestler has always been interested in the few intellectuals who are motivated by the logic of ideas rather than the vast majority of persons who are not. He always conceeded that coercion and terror lay behind the greatest number of confessions, but just as firmly insisted that mere criminality was not the sole explanation. There was, he maintained, a logical element in the nature of revolutionary ideology that needed to be accounted for.

While Koestler's thesis and analysis of modern revolutionary ideology is not entirely destroyed by the arguments of Ulam and

Tucker, for example, they do pose a special challenge. His arguments would certainly be weakened if it could not be shown that at least some of the victims of the Purge Trials confessed for similar reasons as motivated Rubashov. Because Koestler has insisted on the basic historical accuracy of his novel, he cannot really plead that it is simply a logical outcome of ideas inherent in Marxism independent of their actual manifestation. Other writers who detected such totalitarian tendencies in modern ideologies—Huxley, Orwell, Zamyatin, and others—have taken this line, but it is not Koestler's. Here it is important to recall the time frames of Koestler's novels as distinguished from other writers who have placed their totalitarian states in an imaginary future. Koestler's works are basically set in the present. After *The Gladiators,* he immediately returned to the revolution of the present and never returned to an historical setting of that sort. Even in *The Age of Longing,* the reader does not have the impression of a futuristic setting in the sense of Orwell or Huxley. This specific time frame opens Koestler to criticisms of factual accuracy other writers have avoided.

Among the numerous examples of what might be called "witness literature" on the Purge Trials and the decade of the 1930s, there is a substantial body of writing that has tended to agree with Koestler.[27] Walter Krivitsky's *I Was Stalin's Agent,* written two years before *Darkness at Noon* but evidently unheard of by Koestler until after 1941, gives a picture of the trials by an insider that is an almost perfect parallel to Koestler's. In addition, such works as Victor Serge's *The Case of Comrade Tulayev* and Manes Sperber's *The Burned Bramble,* both by ex-party members, give a portrait of revolutionary ideology more suggestive of Koestler than most of his critics. Or it might be said even if the Purge Trials are merely criminal behavior on an unprecedented scale, they did not lack intellectual allies who were prepared to rationalize them on grounds of revolutionary logic.

Ironically, perhaps, it is Merleau-Ponty who provides the best defense of Koestler's thesis in *Darkness at Noon.* When he attacked Koestler's portrayal of Rubashov, he did so not on any grounds of factual inaccuracy but rather on the meaning that ought to be attributed to him and his story. In *Humanism and Terror,* he constructed precisely the argument that one would have to build in order to freely defend and accept the arguments of the party in the trials—that was, after all, the purpose of his essay: the intellectual's defense of Stalin. If he were faithful to the logic of his own arguments against Koestler, it is not an unreasonable inference to assume that in a similar situation he would willingly confess to render a "last service to the Party." In the final analysis, Merleau-Ponty's thesis is no different than Koestler's, except that he sides with Gletkin instead of the innocence of Rubashov.

In addition, support for Koestler's ideological interpretation of the Purge Trials has come from Robert Conquest's massive study, *The Great Terror*. [28] Drawing freely on the work of Koestler and other writers of the period, Conquest has produced the most impressive study to date on the period in question. As such, it carries probably more scholarly weight in the debates than any other single work. Conquest has most decidedly come down on the side of Koestler in the ideological interpretation of a significant part of the trials. Indeed, so persuasive has been the study that it appears to have been a reason why Ulam in a later study of Stalin backed off slightly from his earlier position against Koestler and recognized at least the respectability of the "last service to the Party" thesis. [29] While it cannot be said that Koestler has yet won the debate, if such a thing is possible, it must be said that there is probably more reason to support his point today than at the time he first made it.

III   *Koestler's Critics and the Structure of Scientific Reason*

A second category of criticism has been aimed primarily at the structure of scientific reason that emerges chiefly in Koestler's later works. Most of these critics understand their opposition to Koestler's arguments to be apolitical. In the sense that these criticisms are not tied to advocacy of any particular notion of politics, this understanding is correct. But Koestler himself has been at pains to show that there is a syndrome of ideas about the structure of reason and science that is directly applicable to conceptions about politics. In spite of considerable diversity that seems to separate most of Koestler's critics in the area of science, a closer look suggests that their unity is real; they see Koestler as attacking both reason itself and themselves as defenders of scientific reason.

Koestler's critique of modern science is a noticeable strand of thought that begins in his first work and increases in tempo until his most recent. It is not an attack on science itself, but rather a criticism of what he sees as a perversion of true science. What Koestler referred to as the commissar form of reasoning was always his protagonist, whether in politics or science. For Koestler, there was no substantive difference between them, and at least some of his critics agreed with him.

One of the close links between the political critics of Koestler's interpretation of revolution and his scientific critics is John Strachey. Strachey left the British Communist party at about the same time that *Darkness at Noon* appeared, although there does not seem to be any causal connection between the two events. Unlike Koestler, however, Strachey's departure from the party led to an entirely different series of conclusions. He never seems to have entertained Koestler's doubts about the historical truth of Marxism or the inevitability of the transformation of capitalist society into a classless one. He retained the commissar's futuristic vision even after abandoning the part of the commissar. In many respects he was a very kindred spirit with Merleau-Ponty, except that he is several rungs below him as a writer and philosopher. His basic disagreement with the party appears to have been over the influence of Stalin and not the logic of the revolution itself. He insisted, unlike either Koestler or Merleau-Ponty, that Stalin and the revolution could be kept separate. In his *The Strangled Cry*, posthumously published in 1962, he featured as the lead essay his reflections on *Darkness at Noon* and its impact on scientific reason in the modern world.

In *The Strangled Cry*, Strachey reluctantly admitted that Koestler had drawn a truthful picture of the Purge Trials. He found the truth of this portrait of the revolution to be irrelevant, however, to the larger question of historical truth: "Nobody can today be in the least interested in whether the book is true or not: of course it is true." But if there is no longer any point in denying the truth of Koestler's work, there remains an ongoing need to defend the idea of revolution against Koestler. It is the structure of reason that informed the revolution that is in danger because of Koestler's attacks. The fact that this reason found a home in Gletkin and Stalin could no longer be an issue:

This was the first book to reveal the far reaching consequences upon the mind and spirit of the West in the rejection of Communism. It revealed that Communism could not be rejected without re-emphasizing just those aspects of life which had been least emphasized and not only by Communism. And that might mean calling into question the whole rationalist tradition. The values which the book began to preach were subversive of much more than Communism.[30]

Strachey called *Darkness at Noon* the first work in what he called "the literature of reaction" that has become the hallmark of the postwar world. By this he meant more than a "reactionary" view of

148 ARTHUR KOESTLER

politics, but a reactionary view of science as well. Its scandal and its power, he said, was that it consisted not only of political arguments against the idea of revolution, but against scientific empiricism as well. His conception of scientific reason, as Koestler noted in a rebuttal, was the identification of reason with materialism.[31] Strachey's perceptions were not his alone, but found numerous echoes elsewhere.[32]

Among Koestler's scientific writings, *The Sleepwalkers* drew the sharpest criticism and linked its critics with that of Strachey and political ideology. For example, the essay-review by De Santillana and Drake found most objectionable the Koestler's notion that scientific creativity could not be explained in mechanistic terms.[33] Again, Charles Gillispie's *The Edge of Objectivity* saw Koestler as attacking reason itself when he attacked the notion of a mechanistic science. Gillispie is more charitable in his critique, attributing Koestler's apparent lapse to a misunderstanding, but he basically defends the mechanistic view. In the trial of Galileo, for example, he does not see the issues as a clash between opposing truths, but rather as placing truth on sounder grounds. Koestler's notion of science stands condemned as a poetic understanding of reason that has been superseded: "That way lies surrender of the measure of independence which science by its determined toughness has won for scholarship and thought. That way lies, finally, the unforgivable vulgarity which resents that which surpasses the common understanding, and which ends in . . . darkness at noon."[34]

When Koestler's trilogy on the science of the mind first appeared, it seemed to be more heretical in its ideas than was the case only a decade later. There are a number of reasons for this shift in attitude. Shortly after Koestler began his work, a number of other similar arguments began to appear that reinforced and modified some of his notions. Chief among these studies was the influential and controversial work of Thomas Kuhn, mentioned earlier. As these works developed similar themes independently of one another they gave rise to more fundamental questioning of the notion of "science" even as the specific theses were rejected in whole or part. Within a decade after the publication of *The Sleepwalkers,* the mysterious aspects of creativity and reason itself were again a very lively topic among scientists for the first time in the twentieth century. George Kneller in *The Art and Science of Creativity* and Anthony Storr in *The Dynamics of Creation* gave evidence that the issue of scientific creativity and reason was once more a debatable subject.[35] Without accepting all of Koestler's conclusions, more and more scientists have begun to entertain some of his observations on scientific originality and reason.[36]

IV   *Arthur Koestler and Zionism*

Throughout Koestler's writing there is a recurrent theme of religious symbolism. In much of his fiction, this has taken the form of a reverse Christian symbolism, reminiscent of a gnostic tradition of interpretation. But in addition to his literary manipulation of certain Christian symbols, there is also a highly visible interest in Jewish religious and cultural traditions. This is not surprising given Koestler's origins in East European Jewry. The two traditions are intertwined in Koestler to an unusual degree and have been the source of considerable confusion. The Christian symbolism has already been noted, but the Jewish strain requires separate comment.

Koestler's three main works on exclusively Jewish themes are widely separated over time and are not confined to a single form of writing. They are *Thieves in the Night*, a novel published in 1946 about Jewish settlements in Palestine between the two world wars, *Promise and Fullfilment*, as essay on the Arab-Jewish warfare from 1917 until the creation of the Jewish state, and *The Thirteenth Tribe*, a history written in 1976 about the origins of European Jewry in the seventh through the eleventh centuries. As with most of Koestler's work, all three have been controversial and have embroiled him in disputes within the Jewish community and outside.

Thieves in the Night is probably his least successful novel. This is true in terms both of literary style and of thematic focus in the substance of the work. The central idea is the reverse of his trilogy on the ethics of revolution. In the postscript to the Danube Edition, he wrote of the Jewish experience with anti-Semitism that it had been as devastating on the national character of Jews as on their persecutors. "If power corrupts, the reverse is also true: persecution corrupts the victim, though perhaps in subtler and more tragic ways. In both cases the dilemma of noble ends begetting ignoble means has the stamp of inevitability."[37] At the time the novel appeared, many interpreted Koestler's theme as a harsh criticism of Jews by a Jew. Because the novel was published in 1946, immediately after the Holocaust, Koestler was unfairly subjected to much the same sort of criticism that met Hannah Arendt after her publication of *Eichmann in*

Jerusalem. The criticism was especially cruel because Koestler, as with so many European Jews, had lost virtually all of his family in the Nazi concentration camps.

What Koestler dealt with in *Thieves in the Night* was what he called "the ethics of survival." It was the story of the costs of survival in a hostile environment from the point of view of those who survived. The setting is a Jewish settlement in Palestine called "Ezra's Tower." The picture of the Arab-Jewish war that Koestler gives is far from heroic. It is a petty war of tortures, terror, counterterror, and the gradual contraction of the souls of the Jewish participants. It is a dismal picture that is at odds with any romantic notions of a holy war between right and wrong.

Originally, *Thieves in the Night* was intended as the first volume of a trilogy that would culminate in the peaceful growth of Ezra's Tower. But apparently Koestler decided that the story could not be dealt with in a fictional form in its subsequent development. The result was an essay on the Arab-Jewish warfare that finally culminated with the creation of Isreal. In *Promise and Fulfilment,* published in 1949, Koestler produced a less controversial account of the growth of the Jewish state. There was no basic disagreement with his position in the novel, but because it reflected the other side of the questions he had raised earlier, it struck some as a change of tone.

In *The Thirteenth Tribe,* published in 1976, Koestler turned to a straightforward history of the origins of East European Jewry. He also stepped back into his accustomed position as the center of a controversy. *The Thirteenth Tribe* is a popular history of the Khazar Empire in East Europe from the seventh through the eleventh centuries. Though an unlikely subject for a controversial topic, Koestler turned the history into one of the most intrigueing theses on the nature of contemporary anti-Semitism to be found anywhere.

Most twentieth century Jews trace their ancestry to Eastern Europe. Historically this usually means that they conceive of a link with the Jerusalem of the Old Testament that runs in an unbroken line through East Europe. Koestler, however, argues that these Jews are not Semetic in origin at all. Instead, he says, they are a Turkish people, descendents of Khazars who adopted Judaism out of political necessity rather than religious conversion. Caught in the seventh century between powerful Chrisitan and Moslem empires, the Khazars chose Judaism as a means of diplomatically placing a foot in both camps of their potential foes. When the Khazar kingdom fell apart in the eleventh century, the survivors migrated west into what is today referred to as Eastern and Central Europe. What makes the history so fascinating is the conclusion the Koestler draws from it regarding anti-Semitism:

the large majority of surviving Jews in the world [are] of Eastern European . . . origin. If so, this would mean that their ancestors came not from Jordan but from the Volga . . . once believed to be the cradle of the Aryan race. . . . Should this turn out to be the case, then the term 'anti-Semitism' would become void of meaning, based on a misapprehension shared by both the killers and their victims. The story of the Khazar Empire, as it slowly emerges from the past, begins to look like the most cruel hoax which history has ever perpetrated.[38]

His conclusion logically follows from the misunderstanding of the anti-Semitism. The Jews ought to either emigrate from their present countries to Israel or assimilate with their present host countries and lose their Jewishness. This is less difficult than it might at first appear because Koestler notes that most Jews have long since ceased to believe in God and the theological tenents of their religion. God is dead, and only cultural Judaism survives in Zionism. But even here the differences between Semetic and non-Semitic Jews are more important than their similarities: they "have no cultural traditions in common, merely certain habits and behavior-patterns derived by social inheritance from the traumatic experience of the ghetto, and from a religion which the majority does not practice or believe in."[39]

Much of the controversy over *The Thirteenth Tribe* centered on Koestler's treatment of anti-Semitism and what seemed to many to be a new interpretation of "the final solution." Reviewers tended to be harsh in their criticism, part of it rightly so. On academic grounds alone *The Thirteenth Tribe* is open to a number of scholarly objections. Surely Hilter's crusade against the Jews was more than merely Semitic in origin. Furthermore, by reducing religious differences to a question of quaint behavior patterns, Koestler may have fallen into the behavioral trap he spent so much of his life avoiding and criticising. But it is not an attack on Jews or their religion that Koestler is engaged in, critics to the contrary not withstanding. From first to last, Koestler has been most impressed with the sheer power of modern totalitarian regimes. The comparative weakness of the individual opressed by these regimes rather than the ability of some men to resist seems to Koestler the paramount fact of political life. Given his agrument that God is dead, for modern man anyway, the Jewish tendency to cling to religion in the twentieth century appears as an anachronism at best and at worst another excuse for Jewish genocide.

V Concluding Remarks

The most fundamental organizing principle in Koestler's work, the basis for its unity within a diversity of forms, is the search for a rational source of order in the human condition. That the search is never consumated is due in large measure to the bifurcated notion of reason, symbolized in the yogi and the commissar. The symbolization of order in these terms permits the appearance of a rational analysis of means and ends in the human condition. But the symbolization of a rational world view is not the same thing as a rational order. Koestler's problem therefore turns on which of the two symbols is the most rational—scarcely a choice that is likely to seem reasonable to most people given the ends to which both inevitably lead.

It does not seem unreasonable, therefore, to conclude that the bottom line of Koestler's understanding of the human condition is the irrationality of that condition. It might be possible here to draw a parallel between Koestler and Camus. Both have made a distinction between rebellion and revolution. But even further, both see the rebel as a person who is affirming his personal worth against a deaf and dumb universe. In Koestler, however, the absurdity of the universe can be matched by a politicized solution. Reason in Koestler's scheme of things stands or falls by its ability to offer a way out of man's predicament. In other words, the ultimate use of reason is its political utility.

The problem with reason thus conceived is that its application in politics only serves to further reveal the absurdity of the human condition. In Koestler's work, fiction as well as nonfiction, the reader is most often presented with the specter of reason failing to triumph, especially if that reason is at all linked to morality. This is as true of Spartacus as of Galileo. The occasional triumphs of reason are almost exclusively of the mind. The new, rational praxis based on modern scientific reason seems to be as much an illusion in *The Call-Girls* as it was in *The Gladiators*. Within such a context, reason takes on the attributes of a divine joke—all it can do is to expose the futility and final absurdity of the human condition.

Though the characters in Koestler's fiction are engaged in a mighty effort to break free of this irrationality, they never make it. The result is a pessimism in his work that has been one of its most often noted characteristics. Yet Koestler is not ultimately pessimistic. There is a strong spiritual side to his writing that also shines through at some of the most unexpected times. The presence of spirit is never wholly absent. There is no resolution to these conflicts in the human condition for Koestler, but they are described as vividly and as dramatically as anywhere in modern literature.

Notes and References

Chapter One

1. Arthur Koestler, in *The God That Failed* (New York, 1949), p. 17.
2. Arthur Koestler, *The Act of Creation* (Danube Edition, 1969), p. 258.

Chapter Two

1. In Richard Crossman, ed., *The God That Failed* (New York, 1949), p. 64; George Watson, "Were the Intellectuals Duped? The 1930's Revisited," *Encounter,* December 1973.
2. Stephen Spender, *Forward From Liberalism* (London, 1937), p. 205.
3. Hans Meyerhoff, "Farewell to Politics," *Commentary,* June 1956. Meyerhoff wrote: "Koestler is not, as he would like us to believe, the lone prophet crying in the wilderness; he is like the rest of us. His talent has always been to dramatize his own life as if it were the march of history."
4. "The Dilemma of Our Time: Noble Ends and Ignoble Means," *Commentary,* June 1946, pp. 1–2.
5. *Arrow in the Blue* (Danube Edition, 1969), p. 319.
6. Karl Marx, "Theses on Feuerbach," in Robert Tucker, ed., *The Marx-Engels Reader* (New York, 1972), p. 109.
7. Lenin, "The State and Revolution," in Robert Tucker, ed., *The Lenin Anthology* (New York, 1975), p. 334.
8. *The Yogi and the Commissar* (Danube Edition, 1965), p. 98.
9. "Dilemma of Our Time," p. 2.
10. *Yogi and Commissar,* pp. 15–25.
11. *Ibid.,* p. 16.
12. *Arrow in the Blue,* p. 15.
13. *The Trail of the Dinosaur* (Danube Edition, 1970), pp. 7–8, 1946.
14. *Ibid.,* p. 7.
15. John Atkins has written: "In his heart Koestler remains a Communist, but his Communism is the pristine variety of the theorists, not the distinct sample displayed by Soviet Russia." *Arthur Koestler* (London, 1956), p. 42.
16. *Trail of the Dinosaur,* p. 128.
17. *Yogi and Commissar,* p. 207.
18. *The Invisible Writing* (Danube Edition, 1970), p. 41.

154

19. *Trail of the Dinosaur*, pp. 128–41.
20. *Arrow in the Blue*, pp. 307–13.
21. *Trail of the Dinosaur*, p. 140.
22. *The God That Failed*, p. 17.
23. *Drinkers of Infinity* (London, 1968), p. 188.
24. *The God That Failed*, p. 16.

Chapter Three

1. On this point see Robert Gorham Davis, "The Sharp Horns of Koestler's Dilemma," *The Antioch Review*, Winter 1944–1945.
2. *The Gladiators* (Danube Edition, 1965), p. 14.
3. *Ibid.*, p. 69.
4. *Ibid.*, p. 70.
5. *Ibid.*, p. 71.
6. *Ibid.*, p. 74.
7. Koestler's symbolism here is strikingly similar to modern gnosticism. On classical gnosticism, see Hans Jonas, *The Gnostic Religion* (Boston, 1958); on modern gnostic movements, see Eric Voegelin, *The New Science of Politics* (Chicago, 1952).
8. *Invisible Writing*, pp. 319–27.
9. *Gladiators*, p. 115.
10. *Ibid.*, p. 130.
11. *Ibid.*, p. 151.
12. *Ibid.*, p. 194.
13. *Ibid.*, p. 202–3.
14. *Ibid.*, p. 207.
15. *Ibid.*, p. 216.
16. *Ibid.*, p. 235.
17. *Ibid.*, p. 279.
18. *Ibid.*, p. 291.
19. *Ibid.*, p. 319.
20. *Ibid.*, p. 297.
21. *Ibid.*, p. 308.

Chapter Four

1. Arthur Koestler, *Darkness at Noon* (Danube Edition, 1973), p. 82.
2. *Ibid.*, pp. 89, 93.
3. *Ibid.*, pp. 102–3.
4. *Ibid.*, pp. 99–100.
5. *Ibid.*, p. 248.
6. *Ibid.*, p. 254.
7. *Ibid.*, p. 77.
8. *Ibid.*, p. 49.
9. *Ibid.*, p. 90.
10. For an excellent discussion of the "grammatical fiction", see Gronwy

Rees, "*Darkness at Noon* and the 'Grammatical Fiction' ", in Harold Harris, ed. *Astride the Two Cultures–Arthur Koestler at 70* (New York, 1976).

   11. On the opposition of the "We" to the "I", a suggestive novel that may have influenced Koestler on this point is Yevgny Zamyatin, *We* (New York, 1970).

   12. *Darkness at Noon*, p. 48.

   13. *Ibid.*, p. 243.

   14. *Ibid.*, p. 62–63.

   15. *Ibid.*, p. 146.

   16. *Ibid.*, p. 146.

   17. *Ibid.*, pp. 146–47.

   18. *Ibid.*, pp. 178–79.

   19. *Ibid.*, p. 180.

   20. *Ibid.*, p. 20.

   21. *Ibid.*, p. 20.

Chapter Five

   1. *Arrival and Departure* (Danube Edition, 1968), p. 21.

   2. *Ibid.*, p. 22.

   3. *Ibid.*, p. 38.

   4. *Ibid.*, p. 38.

   5. *Ibid.*, p. 42.

   6. *Ibid.*, p. 45.

   7. *Ibid.*, p. 60.

   8. *Ibid.*, p. 70.

   9. *Ibid.*, p. 104.

   10. *Ibid.*, p. 104.

   11. *Ibid.*, p. 115.

   12. *Ibid.*, p. 120.

   13. *Ibid.*, p. 135.

   14. *Ibid.*, pp. 153–54.

   15. *Ibid.*, p. 161.

   16. *Ibid.*, p. 177.

   17. *Ibid.*, p. 176.

   18. *Ibid.*, pp. 182–83.

Chapter Six

   1. *The Age of Longing* (Danube Edition, 1970), p. 13.

   2. *Ibid.*, pp. 30–31.

   3. *Ibid.*, p. 46.

   4. *Ibid.*, p. 128.

   5. *Ibid.*, p. 28.

   6. *Ibid.*, pp. 282–83.

   7. See Koestler's comments in *Arrow in the Blue*, pp. 328–29.

   8. *Age of Longing*, p. 26.

9. *Ibid.*, p. 123.
10. *Ibid.*, p. 22.
11. *Ibid.*, p. 26.
12. *Ibid.*, p. 27.
13. *Ibid.*, p. 20.
14. *Ibid.*, p. 363.
15. *Ibid.*, p. 361.
16. *Ibid.*, p. 361.
17. *Ibid.*, p. 363.
18. *Ibid.*, p. 79.
19. *Ibid.*, p. 81.
20. *Ibid.*, p. 357.

Chapter Sēven

1. *Arrow in the Blue*, pp. 347–48.
2. *The Sleepwalkers* (Danube Edition, 1968), p. 513.
3. *Invisible Writing*, p. 431.
4. *Ibid.*, p. 431.
5. *Sleepwalkers*, p. 522.
6. *Ibid.*, p. 527.
7. *Ibid.*, p. 515.
8. *Ibid.*, p. 537.
9. *The Act of Creation* (Danube Edition, 1969), p. 287. The first edition of this work contains a "second book" entitled "Habit and Originality" that is missing in the Danube Edition.
10. *Ibid.*, p. 289.
11. *Yogi and Commissar*, p. 222.
12. See Carl B. Hausman, "Understanding and the Act of Creation," *Review of Metaphysics*, September 1966.
13. *Drinkers of Infinity*, p. 213.
14. *The Ghost in the Machine* (London, 1969), pp. 47–48.
15. *Ibib.*, p. 48.
16. *Ibid.*, p. 56.
17. *Ibid.*, p. 57.
18. *Gladiators*, p. 130.
19. *Ghost in the Machine*, pp. 338–39.
20. *Ibid.*, pp. 326–27.
21. *Ibid.*, p. 327.
22. *Ibid.*, p. 336.
23. *Ibid.*, pp. 337–38.
24. "A Conversation with Arthur Koestler," *Psychology Today*, January 1970, p. 84.
25. Arthur N. Gilbert, "Pills and the Perfectability of Man," *The Virginia Quarterly Review*, Spring 1969, p. 326.

26. *Reflections on Hanging* (Danube Edition, 1970), p. 249.
27. *Drinkers of Infinity*, p. 152.

Chapter Eight

1. *The Call-Girls* (London, 1972), p. 40.
2. *Ibid.*, p. 45.
3. *Ibid.*, p. 92.
4. *Ibid.*, p. 34.
5. *Ibid.*, p. 36.
6. *Ibid.*, pp. 62–64.
7. *Ibid.*, p. 49.
8. *Ibid.*, p. 138.
9. *Ibid.*, p. 78.
10. *Ibid.*, p. 142.
11. *Ibid.*, pp. 112–13.
12. *Ibid.*, p. 127.
13. *Ibid.*, p. 108.
14. *Ibid.*, p. 111.
15. *Ibid.*, p. 84.
16. *Ibid.*, p. 115.
17. *Ibid.*, p. 117.
18. *Ibid.*, p. 118.
19. *Ibid.*, p. 66.
20. *Ibid.*, p. 130.
21. *Ibid.*, p. 132.
22. *Ibid.*, p. 135.
23. *Ibid.*, p. 137.
24. *Ibid.*, p. 137.
25. *Ibid.*, p. 140.
26. *Ibid.*, p. 140.
27. *Ibid.*, p. 179.
28. *Ibid.*, pp. 163-64.
29. *Ibid.*, p. 182.
30. *Ibid.*, p. 184.

Chapter Nine

1. Manes Sperber, "Koestler il y a vingt ans", in Pierre Debray-Ritzen, *Arthur Koestler*. Paris: Editions de l'Herne, 1975.
2. George Orwell, *Nineteen Eighty-Four* (New York, 1949), p. 80.
3. Two notable exceptions to this are Raymond Mortimer, "Arthur Koestler", *The Atlantic Monthly*, November 1946; and V. S. Pritchett's essay "Koestler: A Guilty Figure", in *Books in General* (London, 1953).
4. David Caute, *Communism and the French Intellectuals* (New York, 1964).

5. *Invisible Writing*, pp. 490-92.

6. François Goguel, "Géographie du Referendum et des elections de mai-juin 1946", *Esprit*, année 14, juillet 1946; Remy Rourk, "Le sens du referendum", *Le Monde*, 7 mai 1946; J.-F. Compeyrot, "Majorité Politique", *Révue Politique et Parlementaire*, 48e année, 10 mai 1946.

7. Roger Garaudy, *Literature of the Graveyard*. New York, 1948, p. 50.

8. *Ibid.*, p. 55.

9. Roger Garaudy, *Marxism in the Twentieth Century*. New York, 1970, esp. p. 153.

10. Caute, pp. 132-33.

11. Leon Trotsky, *The Defense of Terrorism*. London, 1921.

12. Maurice Merleau-Ponty, *Humanism and Terror* (Boston, 1969), pp. 94-95.

13. *Ibid.*, p. xxxii.

14. *Ibid.*, pp. 10, 13.

15. *Ibid.*, p. 29.

16. *Ibid.*, p. 27.

17. *Ibid.*, p. 36.

18. *Ibid.*, pp. 92–93.

19. *Ibid.*, p. 85.

20. See Watson.

21. Issac Deutscher, *Stalin. A Political Biography* (New York, 1949), p. 374; and his *The Prophet Outcast. Trotsky: 1929–1940* (New York, 1963).

22. Alexander Dallin and George Breslauer, *Political Terror in Communist Systems* (California, 1970), p. 143.

23. Adam B. Ulam, *The New Face of Soviet Totalitarianism* (New York, 1965), p. 183.

24. Robert C. Tucker and Stephen F. Cohen, eds., *The Great Purge Trial* (New York, 1965), p. XLI.

25. Stephen F. Cohen, *Bukharin and the Russian Revolution. A Political Biography, 1888–1938* (New York, 1973), pp. 337–81.

26. *Darkness at Noon*, p. 253; see also his chapter entitled "Darkness at Noon" in *Invisible Writing*, pp. 478–94.

27. The single work that most impressed Koestler was the memoir by General Walter Krivitsky, *I Was Stalin's Agent* (London, 1939); also his introduction to Alexander Weissberg, *The Accused* (New York, 1951).

28. Robert Conquest, *The Great Terror. Stalin's Purge of the Thirties* (New York, 1968), esp. p. 189.

29. Adam B. Ulam, *Stalin. The Man and His Era* (New York, 1973), esp. p. 410.

30. John Strachey, *The Strangled Cry* (London, 1962), p. 14.

31. *Drinkers of Infinity*, pp. 284–86.

32. Irving Howe, *Politics and the Novel* (New York, 1957); and Pritchett.

33. Giorgio de Santillana and Stillman Drake, "Arthur Koestler and his Sleepwalkers," *Isis*, 50 (September 1959).

34. Charles Coulston Gillispie, *The Edge of Objectivity. An Essay in the History of Scientific Ideas* (Princeton, 1960), p. 53.

35. George F. Kneller, *The Art and Science of Creativity* (New York, 1965); Anthony Storr, *The Dynamics of Creation* (London, 1972).

36. Pierre Debray-Ritzen, "Trois entretiens sur Arthur Koestler," in *Arthur Koestler* (Paris, 1975); see also Harris.

37. *Thieves in the Night* (Danube Edition, 1965), p. 335.

38. *The Thirteenth Tribe. The Khazar Empire and Its Heritage* (New York, 1976), p. 17.

39. *Ibid.*, pp. 225-226.

Selected Bibliography

PRIMARY SOURCES

This bibliography of Arthur Koestler's writing includes in chronological order all of the material used in this study. Additional bibliographical material can be found in Harold Harris, ed. *Astride the Two Cultures—Arthur Koestler at 70*. London: Hutchinson and Company, 1975; New York: Random House, 1976. Most of Koestler's essays have been collected and published in separate volumes of his works. A few of his articles not included in these collections are listed here. Almost all of Koestler's writing has been reissued by his British publisher (Hutchinson and Company) and his American publisher (The Macmillan Company) in a uniform set known as the Danube Edition. A separate citation for the British and American editions of the Danube Edition is not listed here. In some cases the Danube Edition of his works changed the title of the original, bound two works together, or abridged the original work. Where applicable, these changes are noted below. Whenever possible the Danube Edition has been used in this study and all references, unless otherwise noted, are to this edition.

Spanish Testament. London: Victor Gollancz, 1937; abridged as *Dialogue With Death*. Danube Edition, 1966.
The Gladiators. New York: The Macmillan Company, 1939; Danube Edition, 1965.
Darkness at Noon. New York: The Macmillan Company, 1941; Danube Edition, 1973.
Scum of the Earth. London: Victor Gollancz, 1941; Danube Edition, 1968.
Arrival and Departure. London: Jonathan Cape, 1943; Danube Edition, 1968.
"The Intelligentsia," *Partisan Review*, Summer 1944, vol XI, pp. 265-77.
The Yogi and the Commissar. New York: The Macmillan Company, 1945; Danube Edition, 1965.
Twilight Bar. New York: The Macmillan Company, 1945. "The Dilemma of Our Times: Noble Ends and Ignoble Means," *Commentary*, June 1946, vol. XXV, pp. 1-3.
Thieves in the Night. New York: The Macmillan Company, 1946; Danube Edition, 1965.

"The Novelist Deals with Character," *The Saturday Review of Literature*, January 1, 1949, vol. XXXII, pp. 7-8, 30-31.

The God That Failed. New York: Harper, 1949. With Ignazio Silone, Stephen Spender, Richard Wright, Louis Fischer, and André Gide. Edited by Richard Crossman.

Insight and Outlook. New York: The Macmillan Company, 1949.

Promise and Fulfilment: Palestine 1917-1949. New York: The Macmillan Company, 1949.

"Appalling Alternatives," *The Saturday Review of Literature,* January 13, 1951, vol. XXXIV, pp. 19-21, 94-95.

The Age of Longing. New York: The Macmillan Company, 1951; Danube Edition, 1970.

Arrow in the Blue. New York: The Macmillan Company, 1952; Danube Edition, 1969.

The Invisible Writing. New York: The Macmillan Company, 1954; Danube Edition, 1970.

The Trail of the Dinosaur, and Other Essays. New York: The Macmillan Company, 1955; bound with *Reflections on Hanging.* Danube Edition, 1970.

Reflections on Hanging. London: Victor Gollancz, 1956; bound with *The Trail of the Dinosaur, and Other Essays.* Danube Edition, 1970.

The Sleepwalkers: A History of Man's Changing Vision of the Universe. New York: The Macmillan Company, 1959; Danube Edition, 1968; abridged version *The Watershed: A Biography of Johannes Kepler.* Garden City, New York: Anchor Books, 1960.

"Last of the Saints," *Commentary,* February 1960, vol. XXIX, pp. 141-49.

The Lotus and the Robot. New York: The Macmillan Company, 1961; Danube Edition, 1966.

(Editor) *Suicide of a Nation? An Inquiry Into the State of Britain Today.* London: Hutchinson and Company, 1963; New York: The Macmillan Company, 1964.

The Act of Creation. New York: The Macmillan Company, 1964; abridged Danube Edition, 1969.

"Evolution and Revolution in the History of Science," *Encounter,* December 1965, vol. XXV, pp. 32-38.

The Ghost in the Machine. New York: The Macmillan Company, 1967.

Drinkers of Infinity. Essays 1955-1967. London: Hutchinson and Company, 1968; New York: The Macmillan Company, 1969.

(Editor, with J. R. Smythies) *Beyond Reductionism: New Perspectives in the Life Sciences.* New York: The Macmillan Company, 1970.

"A Conversation with Arthur Koestler," Interview by Elizabeth Hall, *Psychology Today,* June 1970, vol. IV, pp. 83-85.

The Case of the Midwife Toad. London: Hutchinson and Company, 1971; New York: Random House, 1972.

The Roots of Coincidence. New York: Random House, 1972.

The Call Girls. London: Hutchinson and Company, 1972; American edition issued without two short stories, New York: The Macmillan Company, 1972.

(With Sir Alister Hardy and Robert Harvie) *The Challenge of Chance.* New York: Random House, 1973.

The Heel of Achilles. Essays 1968-1973. London: Hutchinson and Company, 1974; New York: The Macmillan Company, 1975.

The Thirteenth Tribe. The Khazar Empire and Its Heritage. New York: The Macmillan Company, 1976.

SECONDARY SOURCES

1. Selected Criticism of Arthur Koestler's Writing. This list includes the major book-length studies and references, but only a sample of the many articles. The most complete bibliography of articles on Koestler's novels can be found in Irving Adelman and Rita Dworkin. *The Contemporary Novel. A Checklist of Critical Literature on the British and American Novel Since 1945.* Metuchen, New Jersey: The Scarecrow Press, 1972, pp. 305-308. There is no complete bibliography of articles dealing with his other works, but an excellent source for many such articles can be found in Harold Harris, ed. *Astride the Two Cultures—Arthur Koestler at 70.* London: Hutchinson and Company, 1975; New York: Random House, 1976.

ATKINS, JOHN. *Arthur Koestler.* London: Neville Spearman, 1956. A flawed analysis due in large part because Koestler's writing career shifted direction at about the time the study was completed. Absence of footnotes and citations makes the study difficult to use.

BEUM, ROBERT. "Epigraphs for Rubashov: Koestler's Darkness at Noon," *The Dalhousie Review,* Spring 1962, vol. XLII, pp. 86-91. One of the better essays on *Darkness at Noon.*

BUTTERFIELD, HERBERT. "Introduction" to Arthur Koestler's *The Sleepwalkers.* Danube Edition, 1968. Spirited defense of Koestler's scientific history by one of the foremost historians of modern science.

CALDER, JENNI. *Chronicles of Conscience. A Study of George Orwell and Arthur Koestler.* London: Martin Secker & Warburg, 1968. A sometimes adequate, but generally superficial comparison of the two writers. The author's strong bias in favor of Orwell sometimes leads to a depreciation of Koestler's work.

CROSSMAN, RICHARD. ed. *The God That Failed.* New York: Harper, 1949. A fine collection of first-person essays that is the best work available on writers of the "Red Decade", as directly related to Koestler.

DAVIS, ROBERT GORHAM. "The Sharp Horns of Koestler's Dilemma," *The Antioch Review,* Winter 1944-1945, vol. 4, pp. 503-17. One of the early attempts to understand Koestler in a non-polemical manner.

DE BEAUVOIR, SIMONE. *Les Mandarins.* Paris: Gallimard, 1954; *The Mandarins.* Cleveland, Ohio: The World Publishing Company, 1960. A supurb *roman à clef*, a fictionalized debate between Koestler, Jean Paul Sartre, Albert Camus, and others, on the challenge of Communism after World War II. As one would expect from the acid dipped pen of Sartre's mistress, Koestler does not emerge from the novel in the best light.

DEBRAY-RITZEN, PIERRE. *Arthur Koestler*. Paris: Editions de l'Herne, 1975. One of the best and most indispensible collections of essays on Koestler available. Contains a broad spectrum of French reaction to Koestler.

DE SANTILLANA, GIORGIO, and Stillman Drake. "Arthur Koestler and His Sleepwalkers," *Isis*, September 1959, vol. 50, pp. 255-260. A highly critical and influential essay review of *The Sleepwalkers*.

DRUCKER, H. M. *The Political Uses of Ideology*. London: The Macmillan Press, 1974. Highly negative reading of *Darkness at Noon* from the perspective of the "New Left."

GARAUDY, ROGER. "The Lie in Its Pure State: Arthur Koestler," in *Literaure of the Graveyard*. New York: International Publishers, 1948. The official Communist response to Koestler. Unimaginative and predictable in its critique.

GILBERT, ARTHUR N. "Pills and the Perfectability of Man," *The Virginia Quarterly Review*, Spring 1969, vol. 45, pp. 315-28. A very fine critique of one of Koestler's least commendable ideas.

GILLISPIE, CHARLES COULSTON. *The Edge of Objectivity. An Essay in the History of Scientific Ideas*. Princeton: Princeton University Press, 1960. Conventional history of science before the impact of Thomas Kuhn. Brief critical reference to Koestler's theory, but sympathetic at the same time.

GROSSMAN, EDWARD. "Koestler's Jewish Problem," *Commentary*, December 1976, vol 62, pp. 59-64. The best review of *The Thirteenth Tribe*. Critical of Koestler's scholarship.

HARRIS, HAROLD, ed. *Astride the Two Cultures—Arthur Koestler at 70*. London: Hutchinson and Company, 1975. The best collection of essays on Koestler. Indispensible to any student of his works, fiction and non-fiction alike.

HAUSMAN, CARL B. "Understanding and the Act of Creation," *Review of Metaphysics*, September 1966, vol. XX, pp. 88-112. Insightful attempt to understand Koestler's *Act of Creation* on its own terms.

HAYMAN, RONALD. "The Hero as Revolutionary: An Assessment of Arthur Koestler's Novels," *The London Magazine*, December 1955, vol. II, pp. 56-68. An interesting, though quite critical, perspective.

HICKS, GRANVILLE. "Arthur Koestler and the Future of the Left," *The Antioch Review*, Summer 1945, vol. V, pp. 212-223. A landmark essay in the changing attitudes of the American Left toward the Soviet Union.

HOFFMAN, FREDERICK J. "Darkness at Noon: The Consequences of Secular Grace," *The Georgia Review*, Fall 1959, vol. XIII, pp. 331-45. One of the premier essays on the novel.

HOWE, IRVING. *Politics and the Novel*. New York: The Horizon Press, 1957.

Brief, hostile, reference to Koestler from the perspective of the American Left.

KNELLER, GEORGE F. *The Art and Science of Creativity*. New York: Holt Rinehart & Winston, 1965. A landmark study. One of the first to take Koestler's perspective seriously as an attempt to understand creativity in man.

MEDAWAR, SIR P. B. *The Art of the Soluble*. London: Methuen, 1967. Highly critical of Koestler's science.

MERLEAU-PONTY, MAURICE. *Humanism and Terror*. Boston: Beacon Press, 1969. Originally published in 1947, this is still the most interesting critique of *Darkness at Noon* and defense of Stalin by the French Left. Merleau-Ponty is one of the most important French philosophers of the twentieth century.

MEYERHOFF, HANS. "Farewell to Politics," *Commentary*, June 1956, vol. 21, pp. 596-98. One of the best, brief reviews of Koestler's work.

MOSELEY, EDWIN M. *Pseudonyms of Christ in the Modern Novel*. Pittsburg: University of Pittsburg Press, 1962. A brief discussion of religious symbolism in Koestler's novels.

NOTT, KATHLEEN. "Koestler and His Critics," *Encounter*, February 1968, vol. XXX, pp. 76-81. A spirited, common-sense defense of Koestler.

ORWELL, GEORGE. "Arthur Koestler", in *Critical Essays*. London: Secker & Warburg, 1954. Originally written in 1944, this essay can be found in numerous collections of Orwell's works. It remains one of the most insightful of all essays on Koestler.

PRITCHETT, V. S. *Books in General*. London: Chatto and Windus, 1953. Contains an unflattering essay on Koestler.

RIVETT, KENNETH. "In Defense of Arthur Koestler," *The Australian Quarterly*, September 1947, vol. XIX, pp. 90-94. An early defense of Koestler from his critics on the Left.

ROTHMAN, N. L. "Three Stages of the Soviet Mind," *The Saturday Review of Literature*, May 24, 1941, vol. XXIV, p. 7. Perhaps the most insightful contemporary review of *Darkness at Noon*.

RÜHLE, JÜRGEN. *Literature and Revolution. A Critical Study of the Writer and Communism in the Twentieth century*. New York: Praeger, 1969. Contains an especially useful interpretation of *The Age of Longing* in which Rühle identifies the fictional characters with their real counterparts. Also identifies the characters in De Beauvoir's *Les Mandarins*.

STORR, ANTHONY. *The Dynamics of Creation*. London: Antheneum, 1972. Brief reference to Koestler's contributions in the understanding of the creative act.

STRACHEY, JOHN. *The Strangled Cry*. London: The Bodley Head, 1962. A critique of Koestler by an ex-Communist who continued to defend materialism as a philosophy.

SWINGEWOOD, ALAN. *The Novel and Revolution*. New York: Barnes and

Noble, 1975. New Left polemic against Koestler's view of the dilemma of revolutionary ethics.

TOULMIN, STEPHEN. "Koestler's Act of Creation," *Encounter*, July 1964, vol. XXIII, pp. 58-70. Sympathetic, yet critical essay on Koestler's science of creativity.

2. Selected Background and Reference Works.

Any attempt to place Arthur Koestler in perspective must take cognizance of the attraction totalitarian movements have had on intellectuals in the twentieth century. The literature on the subject is overwhelming. The following list is not intended for the specialist, but rather for the student. These are the works that have, in one way or another, been most influential and suggestive in this study.

AARON, DANIEL. *Writers on the Left.* New York: Harcourt, Brace and World, 1961. Very brief references to Koestler, but an excellent survey of the subject as a whole.

ALMOND, GABRIEL A. *The Appeals of Communism.* Princeton: Princeton University Press, 1954. A distinguished social scientist's analysis. Weak on ideological influences.

ARON, RAYMOND. *The Opium of the Intellectuals.* New York: Doubleday and Company, 1957. One of the most insightful critiques available.

BURTT, EDWIN ARTHUR. *The Metaphysical Foundations of Modern Physical Science.* London: Routledge & Kegan Paul, 1932. An Outstanding reference point from which to judge Koestler's approach to science.

CAUTE, DAVID. *Communism and the French Intellectuals.* New York: Praeger, 1964. Useful for background on the French critics of Koestler.

CAUTE, DAVID. *The Fellow Travellers.* New York: The Macmillan Company, 1973. Brief references to Koestler. Useful for the intellectual background of the "Red Decade."

CHAMBERS, WHITTAKER. *Witness.* New York: Random House, 1952. One of the more insightful self-analysis by a former member of the American Communist Party.

COHEN, STEPHEN F. *Bukharin and the Russian Revolution. A Political Biography, 1888–1938.* New York: Alfred A. Knopf, 1973. The best biography of Bukharin. Useful as a contrast with Koestler's partly fictionalized portrait of him in *Darkness at Noon.*

CONQUEST, ROBERT. *The Great Terror. Stalin's Great Purge of the Thirties.* New York: The Macmillan Company, 1968. The definitive account of the Red Terror of the 1930's. A scholarly work that pointedly defends Koestler's interpretation of the Purge Trials.

CROSSMAN, RICHARD, ed. *The God That Failed.* New York: Harper, 1949. Still the best account of the attraction of intellectuals to Communism.

DALLIN, ALEXANDER AND GEORGE BRESLAUER. *Political Terror in Communist Systems.* California: University of California Press, 1970. A generally good study. But lack of emphasis on ideology causes the authors to depreciate the relationship of Communist theory to practice. Brief reference to Koestler.

DES PRES, TERRENCE. "Survivors and the Will to Bear Witness," *Social Research*, Winter 1973, vol. 40, pp. 668-690. A most suggestive article on the motivation behind persons such as Koestler to record their experiences.

DEUTSCHER, ISSAC. *Stalin. A Political Biography*. New York: Oxford University Press, 1949. An early attempt to assess Stalin by an admirer or Trotsky.

FEUER, LEWIS. "Marx and the Intellectuals," *Survey*, October 1963, no. 49, pp. 102-12. An indispensible essay on the attractions of Marxism to intellectuals.

GARAUDY, ROGER. *Marxism in the Twentieth Century*. New York: Scribner, 1970. Written after Garaudy left the French Communist Party. Brief, critical reference to Koestler.

GRUBER, HELMUT. "Willi Münzenberg's German Communist Empire 1921-1933," *The Journal of Modern History*, September 1966, vol, XXXVIII, pp. 278-297. Although the article does not mention Koestler, it does cover Münzenberg's career during the time Koestler was associated with him.

HOFFER, ERIC. *The True Believer: Thoughts on the Nature of Mass Movements*. New York: Harper and Row, 1951. Still a useful source of insightful observations about the appeals of mass movements.

JONAS, HANS. *The Gnostic Religion*. 2d edition. Boston: Beacon Press, 1958. Insightful chapter "Gnosticism, Existentialism, and Nihilism" that places the appeals of Communism in a fascinating perspective.

KRIVITSKY, GENERAL WALTER. *I Was Stalin's Agent*. London: Hamish Hamilton, 1939. More than any other firsthand account of the Moscow Purge Trials, this work parallels the argument in *Darkness at Noon*.

KUHN, THOMAS. *The Structure of Scientific Revolutions*. Chicago: University of Chicago Press, 1962. This influential and controversial essay tends to support Koestler's notions on the nature of scientific creativity.

MEYER, FRANK S. *The Moulding of Communists: The Training of the Communist Cadre*. New York: Harcourt, Brace and Company, 1961. An insightful study of the interior workings of the Communist Party.

MILOSZ, CZESLAW. *The Captive Mind*. New York: Random House, 1951. One of the most insightful studies of the intellectuals under Communism.

ORWELL, GEORGE. *Nineteen Eighty-Four*. New York: Harcourt, Brace and Company, 1949. Still the standard of comparison with *Darkness at Noon*.

SERGE, VICTOR. *The Case of Comrade Tulayev*. New York: Doubleday and Company, 1951. Along with Koestler's *Darkness at Noon*, this is the other great novel of the Purge Trials.

SERGE, VICTOR. *Memoirs of a Revolutionary 1901-1941*. Oxford: Clarendon Press, 1963. The frank memoirs of a Trotsky follower. Close associate of Koestler in early 1940's.

SPENDER, STEPHEN. *Forward From Liberalism*. London: Victor Gollancz, 1937. Written shortly before his break with the Communist Party. Contributor to *The God That Failed*.

SPERBER, MANES. *The Burned Bramble*. New York: Doubleday, 1951. One of the major novels of the "Red Decade" by an author who left the Party over its excesses.

STRACHEY, JOHN. *The Theory and Practice of Socialism*. New York: Random House, 1936. One of Koestler's most unrelenting critics. A good example of the intellectual rot on the Left during the 1930's.

TROTSKY, LEON. *The Defense of Terrorism*. London: The Labor Publishing Company, 1921; reprinted as *Terrorism and Communism*. Ann Arbor: University of Michigan Press, 1961. Both the original title and the subtle change in the reprint speak volumes by themselves.

TUCKER, ROBERT C. AND STEPHEN F. COHEN, eds. *The Great Purge Trial*. New York: Grosset and Dunlap, 1965. Brief reference to *Darkness at Noon* in the introduction. Indispensible for an analysis of the Bukharin trial and the authenticity of Koestler's analysis of it.

ULAM, ADAM B. *The New Face of Soviet Totalitarianism*. New York: Praeger, 1965. Brief reference to Koestler.

ULAM, ADAM B. *Stalin. The Man and His Era*. New York: Viking, 1973. The best study of Stalin to date. Interesting perspective on the Purge Trials with direct reference to Koestler's critique.

VOEGELIN, ERIC. *The New Science of Politics*. Chicago: University of Chicago Press, 1952. Koestler's work tends to give some of the strongest support to Voegelin's thesis that much of the intellectual's attraction to totalitarianism can be explained in part as a form of modern gnosticism.

WATSON, GEORGE. Were the Intellectuals Duped? The 1930's Revisited," *Encounter*, December 1973, vol. XLI, pp. 20-30. The best single article on the subject.

WEISSBERG, ALEXANDER. *The Accused*. New York: Simon and Schuster, 1951. Introduction by Arthur Koestler. A close personal friend of Koestler's. First hand account of the Purge Trials.

ZAMYATIN, YEVGNEY. *We*. New York: Viking, 1972. The prototype novel for many later works, such as *Darkness at Noon* and *Nineteen Eighty-Four*.

Index

(The works of Koestler are listed under his name)